Maker SPACES

Maker SPACES

CREATIVE INTERIORS FROM THE HOMES AND
STUDIOS OF INSPIRING MAKERS AND DESIGNERS

Emily Quinton

Photography by
HELEN CATHCART

RYLAND PETERS & SMALL
LONDON • NEW YORK

SENIOR DESIGNER Toni Kay

COMMISSIONING EDITOR Nathan Joyce

LOCATION RESEARCH Jess Walton
 and Emily Quinton

PRODUCTION Meskerem Berhane

ART DIRECTOR Leslie Harrington

EDITORIAL DIRECTOR Julia Charles

PUBLISHER Cindy Richards

INDEXER Vanessa Bird

First published in 2015
by Ryland Peters & Small
20–21 Jockey's Fields,
London WC1R 4BW
and
341 East 116th Street
New York, NY 10029
www.rylandpeters.com

Text copyright © Emily Quinton 2015
Design and photographs copyright
© Ryland Peters & Small 2015

10 9 8 7 6 5 4 3 2 1

ISBN 978-1-84975-619-8

A CIP record for this book
is available from the British Library.

Library of Congress CIP data has been
applied for.

Printed and bound in China

Contents

zit je net...

Introduction

I have always loved making things and creating spaces that make me happy, and this book came about because I wanted to see how other makers around the world live and work. I believe there is a strong, beautiful and important link between makers and the home and work spaces they inhabit, and this is exactly what I will explore in the following pages.

Over the past few years, we have seen a revival of DIY crafting, combined with exciting advances in technology, all of which have made a huge impact on the ways in which makers live, work and connect with each other and their audiences. Making is a movement, and some argue that it is a shift on the scale of the Industrial Revolution. Increasingly, makers are working from home, using technology to help us do so. Work that once would have required operating from a desk in an office can be done on the move, from home or from the studio.

Strangely, despite embracing the recent extraordinary technological leaps, the Maker Movement has led to the renaissance of craft-based cottage industries, where artisans practising traditional skills use technology as an enabler. Firstly, they employ technology to produce their beautiful work quickly and on a larger scale than they could otherwise achieve, and secondly to enable them to reach a huge audience; an audience that they can communicate with from the sofa or the workbench.

I can see a strong link between the way in which I live in my home and work space, and the making that I do. I know how affected I am by the space I occupy, by the amount of light, by colours, by design and by the things around me, so I was keen to explore this connection between creativity and space with other makers, while celebrating this amazing era of modern makers.

THIS PAGE AND OPPOSITE My own home is a creative, bright and happy space, which I share with my husband and our four children. We all make things every day and enjoy displaying our work around the house to inspire each other and make us smile.

In this book you will see how maker spaces place a high value on methods, materials and process – if you are striving to do work that you value and love, this will be apparent in the way the spaces are constructed and organized. Beauty, craft, homeliness, technology, history and the search for meaningful work can be found in the fabric of how these spaces are made.

As we travelled to locations around the UK, the US and the Netherlands, the same theme kept coming up. 'Our home, our spaces, our work are all a part of us. It is the way makers see the world, the way our brain works,' as jeweller Alix Blüh explained to me. Everyone in this book has such a strong connection to the spaces they live and work in. They all take such care and pride in creating these spaces, whether it is through making furniture and furnishings, painting walls or collecting the perfect pieces for their vision. And they are all affected by the way spaces make them feel. In order to be creative, they need to feel balanced, happy and inspired in their spaces. This means there is much less separation between work spaces and home. We do our craft wherever we are, whatever that craft is, online and off. So the spaces in which we sleep, eat and socialize are also touched by these maker ideas too.

My personal maker space is a family home that I share with my husband and our four young children. My own craft and photography-based making is beautifully combined in our family with my husband Stef Lewandowski's making. He is an artist and technologist, and together we have made a conscious decision to put making and creativity at the heart of our family life. The coming together of art, craft, design and technology puts our family and home (where we live and work) right in the middle of the Maker Movement.

We have a large art cupboard full of supplies that the children can dip into whenever they want to. We make together as a family as often as possible and the children

all draw every day. Our family motto is 'create something every day', and we are at our happiest when we are together, making. But it is not just arts and crafts that we share with the children; Stef also brings his love and knowledge of technology into the home. This is a home of 21st-century mini makers!

If this is the modern industrial revolution, it is also a modern design revolution. I will show you just what this could mean for the way we live our lives creatively, working in beautiful, inspirational maker spaces.

OPPOSITE When you live in a compressed space, like the urban terrace that is our home, you adapt. Our home is filled with dioramas and arrangements of inspiring things that we change almost every week, and help to create them.

ABOVE We start every weekend with one of our epic monster drawing sessions. The children love making as much as we do, and they have their own names for the little gang, 'The Mini Makers'. A little mess never hurt anyone!

Shared spaces

Shared spaces are the accelerators of the Maker Movement. They are co-working spaces where people not only share desk spaces but tools and knowledge too, creating a community of sharing, learning and experimenting. Hi-tech and expensive making equipment like 3D printers, laser cutters, sewing machines and letterpresses are available to people through co-working spaces, paid for by membership fees and donations.

'Fab lab' and 'hackspaces' have started to grow around the world, as well as co-working spaces like the Makeshift Society in San Francisco and Brooklyn. Interior designer and artist Sarah Owen moved across America to begin a new life in Oakland, California, and found joining the Makeshift Society incredibly valuable in establishing herself in a new city. Shared maker spaces are not just about having access to equipment or desk space but they are also places to network, learn new skills and share your own knowledge with other makers.

The makersCAFE, in Shoreditch, London, has been set up by Soner Ozenc to enable people in London to access 3D printers and laser cutters. Soner,

ABOVE 3D printing is coming of age and what was once a pastime of only those in the know is set to become mainstream. Imagine printing with chocolate. This maker space can help you 3D-print a tasty message for a loved one.

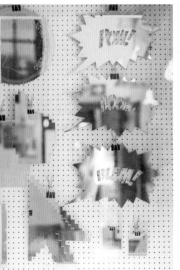

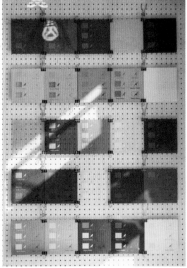

FAR LEFT Anyone setting up a maker space will tell you that the piece of equipment they must have is a laser cutter because with it you can take any digital design and turn it into a physical object.

LEFT 'We are establishing a space where people can come in, grab a coffee, socialize and discuss projects. When they come up with that "brilliant idea", we can help turn them into physical objects,' explains makersCAFE's Soner.

OPPOSITE MakersCAFE in East London symbolizes the shift from old industry to new. The problem with laser cutters and 3D printers is that you have to wait for them to produce the work. So here you can enjoy a coffee and conversation while your creation emerges from the machines. Collaborative spaces like this support the idea of rapid prototyping being something that is conversational.

who runs RazorLAB, wanted to start the makersCAFE to create a space where people can come and discuss their ideas for something they want to have 3D printed or laser cut and then have made in the same space. It is a brilliant way of bringing new technology and digital manufacturing into people's lives in an accessible, friendly and affordable way.

Illustrator Maartje van den Noort discovered the Grafisch Werkcentrum (Graphic Work Centre) in her home town of Amsterdam and loves having a different place to go and work as an alternative space to her studio, where she can work on,

LEFT Making is... whatever you want it to be. The makersCAFE asks its cliental to design a poster as they meet for coffee to discuss their latest ideas. Everything in this space is made locally. Even the lampshades are laser cut in the room.

and experiment with, alternative mediums. The centre has an amazing collection of vintage printing machines, including letter presses, which have been lovingly restored. The idea is that everything in the space must still function; it is not a museum but a working print studio. Many artists like Maartje come to work in the centre and people also come to learn old printing techniques and take

ABOVE The MakerBot 3D printer epitomizes the Maker Movement. What started out as a hobby project is now a billion-dollar business, but it still retains its maker roots.

RIGHT A typographer's dream. When once we might have thought that the age of print was coming to an end, we now see a resurgence in appreciation for these beautiful, hand-cranked printing machines. The printer is the rhythm of the studio.

classes. It is a wonderful way of ensuring that the traditional techniques and skills don't disappear.

However, it is not just physical shared spaces that are so important to today's makers. Virtual shared spaces have completely changed the way that makers around the world can connect with each other, support one another and reach out to their new customers and markets. Online shared spaces have really expanded the Maker Movement across the world. 'The wonderful thing about launching a business in the age of the internet is that you have access to countless resources, guides and mentors. Marketing is now tremendously multi-dimensional and social media platforms can boost your visibility beyond my 1980s wildest dreams,' says jeweller Alix Blüh. Social media creates shared spaces where makers can converse and ask questions, and also share images of their work and appeal to new customers. Pinterest is an incredible resource for finding inspiration and ideas, and Instagram, Twitter and Facebook are also wonderful communities for makers to connect with each

other and with potential customers. Bloggers and magazines can find makers through these shared online spaces, which supports them and encourages them even more. Etsy enables people to sell their products to customers all over the world as well as make the most of the workshops, blog posts, tips and guidance for makers that its community offers. GREAT.LY, an online platform created in May 2014, allows makers to connect with online tastemakers, who then sell their work in individual stores within the GREAT.LY site.

All these online shared spaces can pose some difficulties too. Competition is now global, for example, but there is no denying that the Maker Movement has grown and flourished due, in part, to these extraordinary forums.

Rustic

RIGHT A collection of vintage crates serves as shelves in the kitchen, with clever use of hooks to hang mugs. This arrangement is both practical and beautiful, with the addition of a climbing plant creating a perfect little vignette in the corner of the kitchen.

OPPOSITE Light is cleverly bounced around this dining area with the use of huge mirrors on one wall and windows into a bedroom on the other. A large table, made from an elevator door creates an inspiring space for dinners and gatherings, as well as client consultations.

Beauty laid bare

Artist and interior designer Sarah Owen lives in Oakland, California, in her vast live/work loft, which she created in an old furniture warehouse built in the early 1900s. In September 2013, Sarah put all her belongings in a truck and drove 4,800 km (3,000 miles) from her home in Virginia to start a new life on the West Coast. The transition was made easier by her joining the Makeshift Society in San Francisco, a co-working space for creatives, and here she found an instant community. Since then she has devised the most inspiring, creative, unusual space in which to live and work.

t was the industrial, flexible and open space that attracted Sarah and convinced her to take a gamble and make a brave move across the country. She had in fact only seen the place for five minutes before deciding that it was right for her. Her vision for the space has certainly paid off. 'I always transform spaces and I always enjoy renovating them,' Sarah explains. She looks for spaces with a lot of potential and this one came

RIGHT Here, the dining area looks through into the bright kitchen. This huge, open space has been smartly divided up through the use of different colours and textures on the walls to give them individual character, while maintaining an overall, seamless feel to the whole apartment.

with permission to do with it as she saw fit. 'I've painted pretty much every surface, taken down a wall and stripped it down to neutral,' says Sarah. 'I also had to remove a lot of odd leftovers and create a clean slate from which to build it up from scratch.'

Like a true maker, Sarah has created nearly everything that you can see. She has made much of the furniture, lights and objects out of things that she has found along her life's journey. She used to own a

LEFT This unique kitchen wall has been made from old wooden frames – just some of Sarah's many amazing vintage finds. The frames provide wonderful muted colours and textures against the white kitchen cabinets and white walls.

shop in Virginia, and she brought some of the ingredients for her renovation with her. 'I still have lots of things that may become a tabletop or a lamp for me or a client. I do a lot of installations for homes and interiors. People look to me for interesting and clever ideas for their spaces.'

The amount of space in this loft – 167 square metres (1,800 square feet) – and the fact that Sarah had the freedom to do whatever she wanted with it has really inspired her. She has the space to make a mess, to rebuild furniture, to stretch out and get work done. The building has a huge freight lift/elevator that enables her to bring furniture and supplies up to her space. It also has a great open rooftop for spray painting and messy outdoor projects. Sarah has created a space that is comfortable and liveable yet inspiring and creative. 'I try to maintain a space that looks and feels good, but nothing is too precious or off limits,' she stresses. She loves to constantly change her space. 'Tidying up for a dinner party means making a new table or painting a wall. I just can't help it,' she says with a smile.

ABOVE A workbench is used to display a selection of plants, vintage finds and pieces of art, creating an interesting focal point. It brings together Sarah's repurposing and upcycling work with her fine art and connection to nature.

FAR LEFT This piece is one of Sarah's current installations. The huge metal door creates an interesting background texture for the gold frame and magnets, the latter of which she found in a thrift store.

LEFT This portrait is by Sarah's friend, artist Ian Webb. 'I've re-finished that wall many times, but this paint and plaster recipe seems to be just the right balance of light/dark and subtle/textured,' she says.

ABOVE This large and open lounge area still manages to have a cosy feeling with the use of cushions, greenery, vintage wood and a large wicker basket. All of these are upcycled vintage pieces or repurposed items that Sarah has made.

When you make and collect things, it is very easy to get attached to them. Sarah finds that she goes through phases with the items that she loves, for example a 'nostalgic phase' or a 'purging phase', and her favourite objects rotate. She enjoys living with art, though, both her own as well as other people's. 'Right now, I love the kitchen wall because I had all the pieces and I knew that one day they would find the right spot. When my things come together, it feels good that I have held onto things for so long.' Sarah made

'Tidying up for a dinner party means making a new table or painting a wall. I just can't help it!' she says with a smile.

her bed from the wood in the wall
she took down and her table from
a lift/elevator door. She has a skill
for experimenting, and figuring
out what will go where and work
in unexpected places, creating the
amazing and inspiring feeling that
it was all just meant to be.

Sarah studied at a school of fine
art, specializing in photography, but
when she graduated, she started
to paint. Her father worked as a
decorative arts painter and she began
working with him. She explained
how neither of them knew how that
would turn out but that it went
really well and they collaborated
on some fantastic projects and
installations in the film industry and
theatre, which took them all over the

LEFT A large vintage ladder has been repurposed into a set of shelves for the bedroom to display a collection of books and treasures. The old wood and metal combined with the exposed brick wall continue the industrial feel into the bedroom.

ABOVE The muted grey tone is also found on this antique metal dresser. A beautiful collection of feathers and a hanging piece of found vine bring natural elements into the space and create a charming setting for a collection of photographs.

RIGHT Throughout her warehouse apartment, Sarah has added plants and other natural elements to soften the industrial feel. A rope and suede planter holding an air plant by Craft Carriage hangs on the vintage ladder.

FAR RIGHT Sarah enjoys making things from the unexpected, like her tabletop, which had been the door to a lift/elevator. Here, she has used a hat made from the bark of a coconut tree as an unusual lampshade.

BELOW A simple wreath adorns the white-painted brick wall. 'I made this from the cones of a monkey-puzzle/Chilean pine tree,' explains Sarah. It hangs over a wrought-iron slate stool, again combining the natural and the industrial.

country and overseas. It provided Sarah with an interest in materials and the way things are put together, which naturally seemed to lead to her building a career that is split between fine art and interiors. However, there is a crossover with the materials she uses for both her endeavours. 'I enjoy the combination of the art and the design. When I just focus on the fine art, I miss the collaboration and the design, and vice versa. I like to keep a balance between the two.'

Sarah's move from her home on the East Coast has really inspired her work. The physical space and the weather have been a big influence, but so have the people. She describes the mentality here as 'curious and open' and one in which she has been able to reinvent herself.

THIS PAGE This large master bedroom also has the luxury of a reading area with cosy seating next to the large window. A deep red rug and blue cushions add flashes of colour to this area of the room, while the large, low coffee table provides a wonderful space to display books.

Above

TOP LEFT Small vintage glass bottles are used to hold pens, pencils, paintbrushes and pretty dried flowers. They are both practical as well as inspiring to look at.

TOP CENTRE A large, deep green plant almost looks like a painting in its own right against the plain white wall. The shapes and strong structure sit perfectly in this industrial setting.

TOP RIGHT Sarah's paintbrushes are artfully arranged in this stand, their colours echoing her colour palette. They are standing ready and waiting for her to use whenever she needs one.

ABOVE LEFT Sarah uses similar techniques in both her interiors work and her fine art, as in this framed patina painting on brass.

ABOVE CENTRE The box frame is treated with metallic paint and contains an intricate bird wing sculpture made from sheet copper.

ABOVE RIGHT A sweet little vase holding a dried allium seed head is ideally positioned in front of these two frames, which link back to the wall of frames in Sarah's kitchen.

THIS PAGE Here, Sarah stands at her gorgeous, vintage drawing table to sketch a new idea. The table sits in the studio area of her apartment, next to a large window that brings in plenty of natural light. The studio is a calm, inspiring place where everything is beautifully organized.

Fit for repurpose

Since moving to Oakland and creating this amazing space, Sarah has been much more active in the design/build side of things. She has found herself helping people, who wouldn't necessarily find themselves in the market for an interior designer, bring their spaces together. She is able to invite them here and then demonstrate to them through her live/work environment how these skills can be applied to their shops, studios and homes. 'I live in my showroom,' says Sarah, beaming.

A meeting of minds

Jewellery designer and owner of jewellery store Modern Relics, Alix Blüh is known for her precious pieces, created to last into the future while having their roots in the past. She lives in San Francisco with her boyfriend, photographer Michael Jang, in a 1908 house bursting with style, elegance and creativity.

ABOVE Alix bought this gorgeous colour photograph in its distressed frame from a funky old used bookstore in San Francisco.

THESE PAGES This room has an industrial feel, softened by the dried flowers. 'I love bringing nature into the house, especially because we live so close to the Golden Gate Park but have no green in our own backyard. I'm always allured by the mosses that grow year round on the trees and love having them in our house,' Alix explains.

FAR LEFT A beautiful slingshot Michael made as a child, with a stone carved with 'Dad' by his daughter, Tali. The stone and the feather are from the beach and woods in San Francisco.

LEFT Alix and Michael share a love of old books and items with a sculptural feel or story to them, like this old iron key sitting on a hand-bound notebook. 'You can sense the life of the object and there is a bit of magic in it,' Alix says.

BELOW This corner represents Alix's love for the natural world, which stems from her childhood. Her father and brother were keen naturalists, as was her grandmother, to whom Alix attributes her obsession with hornet and wasp nests.

A lix and Michael began living together in the summer of 2014 and have been through an incredible journey to bring two powerful visual languages and aesthetics into one space, from Alix's vintage treasures to Michael's black and white photography. The result is fabulous, unique and inspiring, and represents a beautiful, fresh coming together of two individuals. 'It has been so incredibly rewarding for both of us,' affirms Alix.

Like other makers, Alix is incredibly closely tied to her spaces and surroundings. 'Interiors and aesthetics are the pulse of what inspires me daily. If things aren't right in my home or studio, it is like a lack of sunshine for me. I truly start to wilt,' she explains. Having so recently moved from her home of 20 years, Alix reflects that boxing up everything, all her memories, photographs,

OPPOSITE A huge print of Michael's iconic image of Joey Ramone's denim-clad legs combines well with Alix's pieces. 'This is truly a collaboration of the two of us. I bring in the natural and rustic elements, and Michael has the eye for edgy modern and graphic things, and his photography plays an important part in our home.'

ABOVE A gallery wall created by Michael against the bright red of the hallway features both of their work and memories, including a drawing Alix did of Michael's son Woody.

journals and precious things, left her feeling 'so ungrounded and alien. However, moving in with Michael has been an incredible rebirth. I'm at the beginning of a special new journey with him,' she says, delightedly.

Alix grew up surrounded by creativity with two very artistic parents. Her father was a painter and photographer, and he played music. Her mother was a teacher at Alix's school and developed a core study for the syllabus called Enrichment, which was all about craft. 'This class and my whole upbringing taught me so much. Art was such a huge part of my life,' says Alix. She discovered her love for metalsmithing when she was just 12 years old at summer camp. 'I spent every waking minute making jewellery there,' she says nostalgically. Alix was always drawn to making things and she fondly remembers how early her love of interiors started: 'I was so specific about how my room had to be. I collected lots of things and spent hours arranging them.'

She went on to study photography at the University of Massachusetts (UMass). There weren't any metalsmithing

ABOVE LEFT Alix and Michael enjoy injecting quirkiness into their home by using unexpected but often surprisingly useful objects. Here, an old bike tyre is suspended from the ceiling and used as a pot holder.

ABOVE RIGHT Michael bought these oversized playing cards at the artist's fundraiser as a bit of fun for the kids to enjoy.

OPPOSITE Bright pops of green in the open shelves and red appliances bring colour into the kitchen. The bold colours are mirrored in the selection of vintage magazines, which add a playful element to the space.

FAR LEFT This adorable vintage child's blouse is from Alix's collection. This is one of her current favourites and features gorgeous lace around the collar. She loves collecting pieces of lace and thinking of the stories behind them.

LEFT This cushion was made by Alix's friend, artist Laura Zindel, who is well known for her graphite drawings of nature and botanical scenes that also appear on her ceramicware.

BELOW Alix made pretty much everything in her bedroom. 'I am really proud of the bedding I handmade, including the hand-knitted throw. I made the hanging lamp from an old basket that I cut a hole into; I even wrapped burlap twine over the black cord,' Alix says.

ABOVE The larger oval artwork is 22-carat gold-leafed bubble glass with a frame that Alix took a blowtorch to and burned to give it that finish. The other artwork is an antique frame with a deer drawn onto 22-carat gold-leafed glass.

courses there, so she used to go home and work on her jewellery in the evenings. She created pieces with tiny photographs and old pocket watches that she would take apart and mount in polymer clay. By the age of 20 she had her own gallery shows. Sadly, though, Alix was very ill throughout her 20s and by the time she recovered she felt she really didn't have time to study metalsmithing. 'I needed to catch up,' she explains, 'so I found a little course, bought great books and I just got on with it, and within three years I was selling my stuff in galleries.' Alix wisely hired an assistant who had been to a great jewellery school and learned lots from her. 'I was so driven. By 33 I was at the trade shows and selling so well.'

When the recession hit, Alix pulled things back and promoted her own retail store, online sales and commissions. 'Although facing the recession was hard, I felt so much freedom to create things. I had the luxury of not worrying about fitting into the right timeline or collection that selling at trade shows prescribed,' says Alix. Now she believes she has a better quality of life and can work in a really organic and natural way.

In conjunction with her own work, Alix supports other makers in her gallery. 'I particularly love the ceramics work and I love to juxtapose ceramics with jewellery.' Alix has created the most magical studio and gallery space. She built it all from scratch and it was a huge project that continues to grow and evolve. 'I am always adding new layers to it,' she explains. 'This space is so fundamentally tied to my spirit. My sense of place and identity, and my sense of wellbeing and self-esteem are so anchored in this space. It is so profound how special my space is to me'.

The bathroom was a pure collaboration between Alix and Michael. 'I absolutely love the claw-foot tub, and gazing up at the tin ceiling with the chandelier while I bathe makes me giddy with joy. The Gershwin sheet music was Michael's idea and he had it blown up. Of course, I had to get that stark white paper softened, so I attacked it with gel medium and raw umber pigment,' explains Alix.

'This space is so profoundly tied to my spirit. My sense of place and identity, my sense of wellbeing and self-esteem are so anchored in this space.'

Everything in its right place

Above her gallery space sits Alix's small studio space, which was previously overflowing with her worldy possessions while she was moving house. 'I had to really shrink and edit it, but I've made a beautiful sanctuary,' she says, with satisfaction. Next to her workspace she has created a little salon where she can invite clients. 'I run a tight ship of a studio now, but the result is that I have so much more clarity. It's given my work so much creativity and energy; it's been like a rebirth,' she explains proudly.

ABOVE Alix works on a piece of her jewellery in the studio above her gallery. 'I am truly grateful every day to be able to walk into this incredible space to do what I love.'
BELOW There is a common thread to all that Alix sells. 'I have been collecting since I was in my teens, so yes, at 50, I have quite an arsenal of quirky old things.'
RIGHT More of Alix's lovingly presented wares. 'Most of what I sell here is art and functional goods that I'm in love with. I'm drawn to creating an environment that celebrates nature and antiquity, curiosity and humour,' she explains.

Opposite

TOP LEFT A sweet display at the counter in Alix's gallery, including items designed by her friend and fellow maker Kimberly Austin.

TOP CENTRE Beautiful vintage pieces, handmade objects and natural treasures are everywhere you look in Alix's gallery. Here, they hang from a branch.

TOP RIGHT Alix's taxidermy birds and her preoccupation with nature are connected to her childhood. 'If you can't escape it, you end up exploding into it,' she observes.

CENTRE LEFT A small vintage baking pan is used here to display tiny pieces of jewellery. Alix presents everything so thoughtfully.

CENTRE AND BOTTOM LEFT Alix uses old books to display her jewellery. 'Displaying it is a profoundly important part of the journey to its creation,' she explains.

CENTRE RIGHT Alix regards the way she displays her jewellery as doing justice to it and enhancing it. Otherwise, it would be left 'feeling sadly humbled on a typical store fixture'.

BOTTOM CENTRE Alix's tools are also beautifully showcased, almost like works of art in their own right. Her space feels so balanced, inspiring and calm – the perfect place to make.

BOTTOM RIGHT Here, seed heads lie in a pretty ceramic dish. Alix loves to bring the natural into all her spaces.

Above

Alix's desk surrounded by tools and trinkets that she has made. 'I feel very lucky to have such an inspiring work space. It feels magical and that informs my work on a very spiritual level'.

An indoor woodland

Jewellery designer Teresa Robinson lives with her black and white dog Marcelle in a sweet little ranch-style house that was built in 1954 in North East Portland, Oregon. Since moving here seven years ago, Teresa has made this house her dream space and completely changed it from the 'clown house' that she originally bought, with its crazy coloured walls and hideous carpets, into a stylish, sophisticated and welcoming home. The interior has a mid-century modern feel with calm but cosy and warm colours, wooden panels and plenty of lush greenery.

Being in a space that she feels happy and comfortable in is incredibly important to Teresa. 'I am such a visually sensitive person that if things aren't right, then my mental state is really affected by it,' she explains. 'When everything is in line and I feel good about that, then I am happy and able to create.' Passing from one area of the house to the next, you can really feel how she has carefully put the house together over time. Currently her favourite room is her bedroom, which she is finally happy with. 'It feels like just the right balance between being calm and clean, and at the same time warm and cosy,' she says smiling brightly. 'I also really love the wall unit in the living room because putting it together was such a fun project.'

OPPOSITE TOP Teresa is working on this dainty weaving frame, which she keeps in the cute basket alongside. Weaving is one of the most popular crafts of the moment and one that Teresa is happy to embrace. Like many makers, she loves to try new mediums to create with.

Teresa's connection to the revival of the Modernist craft movement is apparent throughout her home. Beautiful weaving hangs on the wall, pieces for a patchwork quilt sit in a corner ready to be stitched together and a small weaving loom and yarn peek out of a basket. 'They are all such great mediums and the movement left such a strong legacy,' says Teresa, 'and I think it's important to try to preserve and continue it, even if I'm just doing that in a small way.'

Both Teresa's parents are artists, so growing up in the Pacific Northwest, she was surrounded by creativity. During her time studying Art at Hampshire College, she spent six months in San Miguel de Allende, Mexico, where she took a jewellery class and became completely hooked on metalsmithing. After finishing college she moved to Portland, where 'I got myself some tools and started making stuff in the corner of the laundry room in the basement of my shared house'. And that is where it all began. Within six months she decided to quit her job and become a jewellery maker.

Her life as a jewellery maker began with Teresa taking little cigar boxes full of jewellery into stores and asking if she could sell them there. This was in a pre-Etsy, pre-social media world and right before the time that the DIY craft movement really

OPPOSITE BOTTOM 'The living room has gone through a lot of changes in the seven years that I've lived in this house, but I do think that it's finally at a place where it feels calm and warm and welcoming,' explains Teresa.

ABOVE LEFT Teresa admits that the kitchen is the least 'finished' part of her house, but loves that the original knotty pine cabinets are still there, and has no plans to change them.

ABOVE RIGHT Teresa was afraid that when she put in the vintage wall unit it would overwhelm the room, but it's done the opposite and made the room feel even bigger.

THIS PAGE The dining room is a simple space. 'The light fixture above the dining table was actually the first thing I bought for the house. I feel like it acts as a nice focal point for the dining room. It's a fairly small space and I wanted to keep things pretty simple in there otherwise,' Teresa explains.

ABOVE LEFT This blue wall provides a rich backdrop for the beautiful wall hanging. 'The wall hanging was an excellent eBay score. I think the woman I bought it from said she got it on commission from a weaver in the 1970s. It's a shaggy beast and I love it,' says Teresa.

ABOVE RIGHT To be found in the back sitting room, this wall is papered in 'Woods' wallpaper by Cole and Son. It's a beautiful connection to nature and to all the wood in the front part of the house.

kicked in. Teresa recalls that 'I was making just the right thing at just the right time. I really lucked out. I got one amazing wholesale order and then everything snowballed from there.'

It is not just her home and studio that Teresa is so clearly attached to but also Portland and its creative community. She describes how she came here 12 years ago because it was a place you could easily fit in as a maker and the cost of living was low. Today, this community of artists and makers has grown up and is still thriving.

The Portland Maker Movement has matured and evolved. People have refined their crafts and are being taken more seriously, not just in Portland but around the world too, thanks to platforms like Etsy, social media and blogs. Teresa appreciates just how important the development of these

ABOVE This large, thick, cosy black and white rug covers the wooden floor in the front living room and brings real warmth to the room.

LEFT The black and white poster is by an artist named Debbie Carlos. She makes large-scale prints of her original photos on plain bond paper. 'I think the scale of them is really great. This one is just weird enough to be perfect,' Teresa comments.

BELOW Plants pop up around Teresa's home. 'I like having plants around to bring a little life and warmth into a space. My favourites are ones that I've gotten as cuttings from friends over the years,' explains Teresa.

OPPOSITE Here is Teresa's bedroom, which is currently her best-loved spot in the house. Soft and cosy colours create a relaxing feel to the space. It is simply decorated and clutter-free, making this a calming place to spend time.

'I was making just the right thing at just the right time. I really lucked out. I got one amazing wholesale order and then everything snowballed from there.'

online communities has been for her work and she has met some wonderful people through it. But she admits that it can also have its downsides. 'As makers, your work and your life are so intertwined. You are a part of your personal brand and you have to work out how to curate that. It can be both a blessing and a curse. I've met some really amazing people, many who have become good friends now, but equally it can be hard to keep up with,' she confesses. Social media results in a lot of comparisons with what everyone else is doing and 'for us sensitive artist types, this can make you a little crazy,' Teresa says with a knowing smile.

Crafting a space

Today, Teresa runs jewellery company Tiro Tiro, which she launched in 2013. This, her third jewellery line, sees her embarking on a period of experimentation and improvisation based on her 15 years of experience. Teresa operates from her converted garage, and what an incredible testament to a maker space it is. 'Pretty much everything in my studio I have made with my own hands,' explains Teresa proudly, 'including this,' she says pointing to the huge beautiful, blue wooden work table she is standing at. 'My spaces are definitely an extension of who I am,' she adds.

ABOVE This dark grey exterior with its bright yellow door gives a stylish look to Teresa's studio in her converted garage.

OPPOSITE TOP LEFT Transforming the garage into a wonderful studio space has been a dream come true for Teresa and makes her happy every time she steps inside.

OPPOSITE BOTTOM Teresa's desk area manages to be ordered, stylish, inspiring and creative all at once. Postcards, posters and magazine cuttings hang together with pieces of jewellery.

ABOVE This long workbench stretches along this wall, making space for plenty of storage. Everything is wonderfully organized, with a place for everything in wooden boxes and ceramic pots.

RIGHT In contrast to her house, Teresa's studio has high ceilings and is light and airy. She likes to feel like she is stepping into a completely different environment to go to work.

Above

TOP LEFT Teresa makes models of her work in wax or builds originals out of wire, and then has them moulded and cast.

TOP CENTRE Everything in Teresa's studio is beautifully set out. Here, jewellery pieces sit in pretty trays next to small potted plants.

TOP RIGHT Beautiful finished pieces of Teresa's Tiro Tiro jewellery collection hang on the wall of the studio ready for their new owners. 'I work primarily in bronze, brass and silver, with a little gold thrown in for good measure,' Teresa explains.

ABOVE LEFT Makers are so good at making storage and function both beautiful and interesting. Here plants also bring life into the space.

ABOVE CENTRE Tools hang on the wall together neatly with a giant pair of scissors, which aren't just for decoration!

ABOVE RIGHT Pieces of jewellery back from the casters and ready for Teresa and her assistant to do all the finishing work.

Opposite

When Teresa started as a jewellery maker, she cut, soldered and filed every single piece by hand, but that way of working is no longer sustainable for her. Working with a caster opens up a huge range of possibilities as far as what she is able to do creatively, as well as in terms of expanding her production capabilities.

Homespun

THIS PAGE The joyful sitting room holds a beautiful collection of patterns, textures, shapes and colours, to make an enchanting space for Donna and her family to spend time in. Donna's own work covers the walls, chairs and floor in combination with the work of other makers.

OPPOSITE A charming cupboard sits in the corner of the living room. This provides the perfect space for a delightful display of natural treasures, candles and vases, all in muted autumnal colours, which sits well with Donna's artwork in orange and brown.

Creature comforts

Designer Donna Wilson is famous for her illustrative knitwear and colourful creatures. Walking from the station to Donna's house is like a walk back in time – as you turn into her road, you enter a conservation area and feel like you have left 21st-century London and stepped into the English countryside of the 1950s. Her house is a detached, three-bedroom Victorian cottage, built in 1860. The land on which the house stands was formerly used to grow flowers that were cut and transported to London flower markets, so it really is a place with a history.

OPPOSITE A gorgeous, light and wide hallway welcomes visitors into this house with open arms. A large mirror bounces the light even more, while the vintage telephone and chairs provide eye-catching details and give a hint about what treats might be inside this home.

ABOVE A Donna Wilson cushion sits sweetly on this Piet Hein Eek chair in the hallway.

RIGHT This bright, white room is the heart of the home. It is the biggest room in the house and the one that gets used the most. 'It's a great room', Donna exclaims 'where you can cook and entertain at the same time!'

When you enter the cottage, you walk into the most welcoming, bright and wide hallway, and you know that you've entered a happy and inspiring home. It's easy to see why Donna fell in love with the house in this hallway. The light fills the space and creates a feeling of curiosity about what else lies within.

The house is double-fronted. To one side is the open-plan kitchen/dining room, where more gorgeous light floods in. The ceiling in the kitchen/dining room is really high as, sadly, the house was bombed during the war, but the lasting, positive effect of this is that it has created a wonderful, spacious feeling in the room. It is full of creativity and colour, and the large Ercol table and chairs in the centre of the dining area give a sense of family and togetherness. Donna's animal plates are instantly recognizable hanging on the side of a kitchen cabinet,

ABOVE Donna's creatures feature on these three trays, which bring a light-hearted element to the corner of her kitchen.

ABOVE CENTRE Donna's coveted plates hang on the side of her kitchen cabinet; these ones are purely for decoration, though.

ABOVE RIGHT This menagerie of Donna's colourful collectable creatures and trees sits on a wooden chair in the corner of the dining room.

while her little boy's toys fill a corner. A cosy chair in the corner is bursting with her knitted creatures, which bring not only rich colours and textures to the room but also a feeling of fun and playfulness.

On the opposite side of the hallway is the living room. This is a darker interior, but the wooden parquet floors found in the hallway and kitchen continue into this room, and of course, so does the colour. It is in this space that Donna's love of pattern and colour really shines. She is a self-confessed pattern addict and she enjoys playing with colours in different and unexpected ways. A wonderful, vibrant clash of the two comes together in this room and is distinctively 'Donna Wilson'.

This is the first house that Donna has owned and she has lived here for just over a year. She is clearly still excited about finally having a space that she can really make her

own and sees her home as an extension of her studio and a place in which she can play and experiment. 'It's really important to play,' she explains, and this house is a perfect space to be creative and spontaneous.

Having her own home enables Donna to express her creativity in any way she wants. The white walls and wooden floors provide her with a blank canvas to which she can add her own colours and textures. 'You can

> 'It's really important to play,' Donna explains, and this house is a perfect space to be creative and spontaneous.

make it as inspiring as you want to and have things around you that have memories attached to them, which is important in creating a happy place and home.' She can hang things on the wall and create a very

THIS PAGE This table and the chairs were an eBay find. 'They are vintage Ercol, and the chairs are not made any more. I love the elegant and tactile cow horn backs,' says Donna. 'Everyone sits around the table to eat, draw, paint or just chat.'

personal home, in a way that wasn't so easy when she was renting.

The first room she wanted to make her mark on was her little boy's room, planning to create an 'inspiring, cosy, weird and wonderful land for him', and she has most definitely achieved that. Going up the stairs and discovering it was a joy, as the whole room is like a magical wonderland, with enormous knitted trees hanging on the walls and a huge wolf sitting on the bed. It is such a special and unique space where imagination and creativity will grow, stories will be told and so many adventures will be had.

This home is alive with 'Donna Wilson' personality in its colours, patterns and textures. Her textiles, quirky creatures and playful ceramics pop up all in every interior, leaving no doubt that Donna is really enjoying making this house her own, creative family home.

Growing up on a farm in the middle of the countryside in Scotland, Donna has been making since she was little. Her grandmother was a really good teacher and taught her how to draw and

ABOVE Vintage cupboards are a lovely way to add charm and character to a kitchen. This one is full of colourful mugs, teapots, glasses and egg cups. Donna has combined her own designs with pretty ones that she has collected.

FAR LEFT Brightly coloured knitted sweaters, that Donna has made for her little boy, are hung on the walls. Hanging them in this way turns them into cute works of art when they are not being worn.

LEFT Large wire antlers are used as whimsical hooks for clothes, hats and scarves, while a huge, friendly wolf sits on the bed complete with his own vividly coloured sweater.

ABOVE Donna's little boy's special bedroom is a magical wonderland with its trees, creatures and bright colours. 'With a child's room you don't have to stick to any conventional rules, so it's much more fun,' says Donna. 'I wanted to make it a fun, creative and imaginative place for Eli to wake up in and play'.

paint. It was always expected that she would go to art school, so it was no surprise when she got a place studying textiles at Aberdeen University.

Then, 15 years ago Donna came down to London to study at the Royal College of Art and has never left. When she arrived in London she was struck by all the colours and patterns and found that they had a big impact on her work, which was originally much more organic and earthy. It was while studying at the College that Donna became fascinated by children's drawings and the way that children draw without any worry about perspective or scale, with a wonderful spontaneity, naivety and their own unique style. It was this that prompted Donna to make dolls, using her own voice to develop her

She planned to create an 'inspiring, cosy, weird and wonderful land' for her little boy Eli, and she has most definitely achieved that.

LEFT The white and grey bathroom creates an air of calm in contrast to all the colour in the house. There is still plenty of creativity in here, with framed pictures on the walls and two plants sitting in the corner, continuing the close connection to the natural world.

ABOVE Donna has put her unique stamp on this little vintage Ercol child's chair by weaving wool around it in three different earthy, rich colours, which beautifully complement the blue bathroom tiles.

individual style. She was then encouraged to sell the dolls, which led her to bring a bag full of them to design and concept store Couverture on the King's Road in Chelsea, London. Within ten minutes of leaving the dolls in the shop, the manager phoned her to place an order. The dolls went on to feature in her final year show at the Royal College of Art, where they all sold. Shortly afterwards, she travelled to Japan with a suitcase of her knitted creatures and returned home with a huge order. Fast forward 11 years and Donna has a thriving business with a small team of staff, and she sells her products around the world.

Reap what you sew

From Donna's home it takes about half an hour to reach her studio in Bethnal Green in Central London. The area is 'a bit rough around the edges, but I really like the vibrance and cultural influences,' she explains. Having a studio in a creative area of London enables Donna to work closely with Shoreditch-based home furniture store SCP, as well as other people and companies in Central London. The studio is in an old factory and Donna works here with her team in a large, open-plan space with high ceilings. There is lots of room to display things, sew and pack orders, and there are materials and patterns everywhere. It is a really practical and inspiring space to work in.

ABOVE Donna sits in her Bethnal Green studio at one of the large work tables sewing labels on her fox scarves. Behind her are piles of her colourful work.

BELOW The capacious studio is open plan with high ceilings. It is like a big white canvas, which Donna and her team have filled with colour and texture.

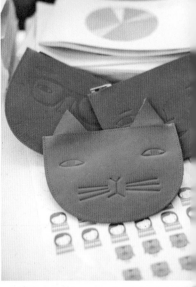

Opposite

TOP LEFT Donna's love for pattern and colour is evident in these three samples of her bright and soft knitted scarves.

TOP CENTRE A crate painted in blue creates a perfect space to store reels of vibrant yarn, tools and a friendly cat.

TOP RIGHT Donna's recognizable faces are made into little leather purses and sit here between sheets of branded stickers and catalogues.

CENTRE LEFT There are two knitting machines in the studio in a small side room. Freshly knitted pieces gather in a cosy pile.

CENTRE A wall is filled with Donna's ever-growing iconic collection of soft toy creatures and trees, creating a cute display.

CENTRE RIGHT These boxes, made from oak-edged laminated plywood, were originally used to display Donna's wares at trade shows.

BOTTOM LEFT A cute cardboard cutout of one of Donna's creatures in green sits in a little corner prompting smiles.

BOTTOM CENTRE Donna's painted wooden people are gathered together to create a colourful arrangement above the rows of filing.

BOTTOM RIGHT Piles of new-season fox scarves are finished and waiting to have their tags sewn on before leaving the studio.

Above

The white walls of Donna's light-filled studio are her blank canvas. 'They let me think,' she explains. 'I love colour but prefer to add accents of strong, bright colour by using patterned textiles.'

Rooms in full bloom

Textile artist Vicky Trainor lives in Northumberland, England, in a delightful 1930s semi-detached house with her husband and two daughters. Vicky has created the most wonderful and special home for her family, filling it with thrifted treasures. When she first walked into the house, she felt like it was home straight away. It is easy to see why. This is a happy, warm and welcoming house, full of character and personality.

LEFT Fresh flowers from the garden fill these vases, creating a pretty welcome to the home in the hallway. The glass cabinet holds Vicky's large collection of vintage china – a lovely way to display such treasures.

RIGHT The sitting room is full of vintage floral finds, from lampshades to sofas, and curtains to framed pictures. 'This is the room in the house that truly hugs you; it is not necessarily about how a room looks but how it makes you feel,' explains Vicky.

LEFT The wallpaper from Anthropologie works
brilliantly as a backdrop in the living room for
all the pieces that Vicky has brought together
to create this living room. It provides a calming
element against the visual liveliness elsewhere.

Vicky loves the 1930s and always dreamed of owning a house of that period. She is obsessed with the late Art and Crafts era, and draws inspiration from Virginia Woolf, Vanessa Bell and the painters of the Bloomsbury Group. Creating her home has been a lovely, slow inventive process, and she feels she has crafted her own 'little corner of the Bloomsbury world.'

Vicky's studio is at the front of the house, while the family live at the back. The living room has a gorgeous, rich and calming colour palette. The wallpaper creates a wonderful feature and the room is full of gorgeous items that Vicky has collected. She is a self-confessed hoarder and

ABOVE Here, the light blue wall is reflected in the blues found across all these floral treasures and like the wallpaper opposite It adds an element of calm to the busy room. Vicky cleverly layers beautiful fabrics, patterns and colours in her interiors in the same way she does in her work.

loves meandering around car-boot/ yard sales. 'I just feel giddy with excitement when I get out of the car,' she laughs, and 'if I see something I like, I bring it home.'

Throughout her home, Vicky has combined items from the 1930s with those from the 1950s, and strong graphic prints with whimsical florals, to create a unique eclectic mix. The theme that clearly joins it all together is that everything stems from the natural world.

Next to the living room is the sweetest little dining room, which leads through into the kitchen. This small room is again full of vintage finds and florals, with fresh flowers from the garden, floral wallpaper and cushions.

'As a family, we spend as much time in the garden as we do in the house. I love to bring the garden into the house and, in the summer, the house into the garden,' Vicky explains. This close connection with the outdoors and the natural is apparent throughout the house. On a sunny day in the summer, 'I will just grab a basket of things and

wander down to the bottom of the garden and work there in my open air studio,' says Vicky.

The whole house is very much a part of Vicky's work and business. Life as a maker means that you are living and breathing creativity all the time and the house is a part of that. There is evidence of Vicky's making throughout the house and projects she is working on are pinned to the walls. She talks about how things she makes for her home can lead to new products or ways of putting fabrics together for her work. Her home is very much a part of her work and her inspiration. You can really see how much she adores this house and she has filled it with things that make her happy and influence her creativity.

Vicky studied textiles and originally designed textiles commercially before she spent time working in the greetings card industry. When she had her daughters, she took a step back and gave herself time to think about what she wanted to do. She gathered all the things she had been collecting

ABOVE Vicky's eye for collecting and displaying wonderful treasures from the past continues into the kitchen. China cups and saucers, jugs/pitchers and bowls are all gathered together. Cake stands overflow with fresh vegetables, while vases of fresh flowers provide a wonderful scent.

'As a family, we spend as much time in the garden as we do in the house. I love to bring the garden into the house and, in the summer, the house into the garden.'

THIS PAGE Vicky's distinctive style is again seen in this delightful, tiny dining room, which has just enough room for a small table and chairs. The room may be small but it is still packed full of character and treasures, demonstrating that you don't need to have lots of space to achieve this look.

THIS PAGE Vicky bought this chest for £12 ($19) in an auction and upcycled it. 'I used six quarter-full pots of different coloured paint mixed together... waste not, want not!' Vicky enthuses. She also likes to use aged maps as interesting covers for the tops of old furniture.

over the years and laid the whole lot out in an effort to find her inspiration. It was through this process that she thought to combine fabric and stationery.

The inspiration for her designs comes from all sorts of avenues, from discovering new colour palettes and designers on Pinterest, to the compositions and images of Angie Lewin and Vanessa Bell. She also seeks inspiration through going on long walks, and finds that being out in the open air with her own thoughts helps to cement new ideas. She loves to collect pebbles on the beach or flowers in her garden and bring them back into the home. 'I like to put myself in my own little bubble, with my own things that I've gathered,' Vicky explains, and that is a perfect description of her whole house.

ABOVE The small family bathroom is a relaxing blue and white, with small pops of colour and a continuation of the floral theme on the bathmats and the vases of fresh flowers.

LEFT This sweet little chair once belonged to Vicky's grandmother and then to her parents. 'I collect selvedges/ selvages from old fabrics and have used them here to re-thread the seat,' says Vicky.

'I like to put myself in my own little bubble, with my own things that I've gathered,' Vicky explains, and that is a perfect description of her whole house.

Bringing the outside in

Vicky's studio, affectionately called 'the linen garden', is a real treasure trove and is bursting at the seams with gorgeous vintage linens, collections of cotton reels, ribbons, lace and bunting. Although it is busy and full, it is beautifully styled, with a place for everything. Her home and studio are special to her because she has the freedom to work from home and be there for her children. She has a relaxed way of working with no specific daily deadlines and finds that having a studio at home gives her time, a happy place to be and her own private world in which to create.

ABOVE When the sun is shining, Vicky enjoys working at the bottom of the garden in her pretty outdoor 'studio'.

RIGHT Vicky uses this corner to plan a display for her next fair. Beautiful vintage bowls wait to be filled and sit together with piles of finished cushions. Box files stand alongside.

OPPOSITE TOP LEFT Vicky isn't afraid of patchworking walls with varied colours of paint or using washing lines of dyed linens or drawing onto the walls. 'This freedom is what I love about the studio,' Vicky muses.

OPPOSITE TOP RIGHT Rows of beautiful, unique bunting made from pieces of vintage fabric and colourful lace hang from the ceiling above Vicky's sewing machine. This table is very busy but there is a place for everything.

OPPOSITE BOTTOM LEFT Vicky's large collection of vintage fabrics are delightfully arranged on the shelves of this old cupboard and also in the drawers. They are all washed, ironed and ready to go, providing inspiration for Vicky's next project.

OPPOSITE BOTTOM RIGHT Rows of beautiful vintage cotton reels in so many lovely colours create a wonderful display, while at the same time being perfectly organized.

Opposite

TOP LEFT Vicky cleverly brings vintage fabrics back to life with these fabulous cushions that she has just made for a lucky client.

TOP CENTRE The start of a stunning embroidery hoop, made from old pieces of fabric, to which Vicky often adds stitched writing.

TOP RIGHT A small cupboard holds colourful lace, ribbons, tiny glass jars and rolls of tape. It is a magpie's paradise!

CENTRE LEFT A pretty piece of floral fabric is draped over the cupboard door along with assorted measuring tapes.

CENTRE Small pieces of vintage fabric and lace are used to create this bunting. Each piece of bunting is unique.

CENTRE RIGHT Pieces of fabric wait to be sewn into something new. Vicky enjoys finding ways to use every section of fabric.

BOTTOM LEFT Old mugs are filled with pens and paintbrushes. A beautiful floral bag hangs on the wall like a painting.

BOTTOM CENTRE Everything is thoughtfully placed and styled, like this vintage floral tin. Function and beauty perfectly combined.

BOTTOM RIGHT These antique ribbons and crochet were brought back to life by hand-dyeing to suit a client's colour palette.

Above

Vicky takes a photograph of the work space every other day to document the changing faces of the walls and tabletops. 'I love that each month it looks so different from the last,' she explains.

RIGHT Inge, her husband and her son always have breakfast, lunch and dinner at the kitchen table when it is just them. They have a plan to make a big, high table in here to work on, which will be 'cooking heaven' for her husband, says Inge.

Heartfelt subtlety

Interior stylist and felt artist Inge Cremer lives and works in the Netherlands in the town of Gorinchem with her husband and son. Their beautiful old 1890s house, with its high ceilings and gorgeous wooden floors, is located right in the centre of the town. This house, which they have lovingly restored inside and out, is an enchanting combination of old and new, and has a wonderfully welcoming and warm atmosphere. It is stylish and beautifully designed, while simultaneously managing to feel comfortable and lived in.

THIS PAGE One of Inge's beautiful felted wall hangings is proudly displayed in the dining room. This is a wide room with high ceilings, so the large wicker light shade and long table work really well. 'We like to socialize with our friends in this room because of the view over the back garden, which we love so much,' says Inge.

ABOVE Inge's home is full of pretty groupings. 'I am always building my collections of things. I find them in shops and thrift stores,' says Inge.

ABOVE A small heart-shaped baking pan hangs on the kitchen wall next to a sweet black chalkboard that is used to write lists of things Inge needs.

ABOVE A recent addition to the kitchen is this vintage door frame, which has been turned into a clever hanging rack.

nge is forever working on her home's interiors. 'My home is always moving,' she explains. For Inge, interiors are a never-ending story. 'I buy things, I get rid of things, I create things. I am always changing things and I am lucky enough to have a husband and son who really appreciate and enjoy this,' she says, smiling. Inge's attention to detail and love for her home are obvious wherever you look, from the cute feathers dangling from her chandelier to little hearts hanging in corners throughout the house. Most recently, the family added a veranda to their outside space and now enjoy spending most of their time outdoors for the whole of the summer.

RIGHT This reclaimed wood cupboard was designed by Inge and made by one of her friends from the wood they gathered together, so it is completely unique. Inge also intends to turn the beautiful vases into lampshades.

The garden, like the house, is beautifully styled and full of fun, bright colours, vintage treasures and sweet corners to explore.

Inge believes that a home and its interiors are really personal and should always come from the heart. She encourages her clients to create a home that is always open to change and one that will continue to evolve. A home should 'move and grow. If it's not right, then let it go and make changes until it is right and you are happy in your space'. Inge has a deep connection to her

LEFT A large wooden chandelier with dangling pompoms and pretty feathers hangs from the living room ceiling. Inge has lots of fun with this chandelier and regularly makes new things to change the display throughout the year.

ABOVE The living room opens into the dining room, allowing the light from both rooms to flood through. Inge has created a cosy corner next to the fireplace, with a bright green chair, a knitted blanket and a collection of candlesticks.

space and the atmosphere within her home. 'It's a feeling I get,' she explains and then laughs, 'Even when we go on holiday, if the hotel room is not right, I make changes!'

After she finished school, Inge studied styling and window dressing, and shortly afterwards she took the next step and became a window dresser and stylist. She worked in that career for 15 years and ran a successful business. She worked throughout the Netherlands, driving around from one town to the next in her car full of props. She clearly enjoyed this time and speaks very fondly of it. She also explored a different creative outlet and worked as an actress for five years. When her son was born she took some time off work to focus on being a mother. 'But my creativity was always there. I enjoyed making things with my son. That was fun, but after three years I also started styling again.'

Five years ago Inge took a felting workshop and totally fell in love with it. 'It's always a surprise,' she says enthusiastically. 'I really enjoy seeing what happens each time and the different, sometimes unexpected, things that can happen with the wool and the soap.' Since taking the workshop, Inge hasn't stopped felting and she now sells her work and takes commissions from clients. She creates very beautiful felt

THIS PAGE Beautiful stained-glass panels have been used in these windows in the roof, which let the light pour into the upstairs landing. 'We really love all the light and space we have in our home,' explains Inge. She has collected different-sized vintage suitcases to create this fun storage solution.

THIS PAGE Inge has designed her bedroom to be her calm, relaxing sanctuary. 'In the bedroom I need some rest, so there is no laptop, phone or television. In the morning, the sun comes into the room, and in the springtime, you can hear the birds singing,' she says thoughtfully.

FAR LEFT One of Inge's many collections of hearts that she displays around her home and garden. Creating, working and living your life from your heart is very important to Inge.

LEFT A gorgeous floral display composed of a painting, a tiny framed image, a postcard, a jug/pitcher of flowers from the garden and two freshly picked blooms taped to the wall.

BELOW Inge found this pink chair at a thrift store and has combined it with more practical drawers. 'I love the handmade roses on it,' she explains. 'I like to mix and match my style. If it feels good, then it works for me.'

interiors, including making objects like large wall hangings and felted seat covers. Once, she even felted a sheepskin.

Today, Inge combines her felt work with her interior styling. She also loves to inspire others to work with felt through her blog and social media. As well as enjoying inspiring others, Inge particularly loves discovering inspiration in nature, magazines, in places she visits and on blogs and social media. 'I also like to step away from all the inspiration, particularly on social media and blogs, so that I can make my own ideas and things,' explains Inge. 'I want to create and make things from my heart.'

When Inge talks about her home, interiors, styling, felting and making, she always emphasizes the importance of creativity coming from the heart. As you walk around her home and garden there are little collections of hearts wherever you go – adorable reminders of the motto she lives, works and inspires others by.

Colour under the eaves

The attic is the most beautiful part of the house for Inge. 'It's where all my creativity starts,' she declares. It is a huge space, packed full of colour, creativity, boxes of vintage treasures, baskets of Playmobil figures, hundreds of balls of wool and piles of vibrant fabrics and magazines. When asked about the toys, Inge laughs and says, 'I just love to add fun to my work, to add little jokes into my felting.' Inge is so content and at home up in her attic studio. It is her special place for making, her haven. 'I need to create. I am always making things. I just can't help it. When I can't create, I get really grumpy,' Inge chuckles.

OPPOSITE TOP This corner of Inge's studio is a cosy area for dreaming up new ideas. A vintage metal daybed is covered with a handmade crocheted blanket and cushions, and large piles of magazines and books wait to be used for inspiration.

OPPOSITE BOTTOM LEFT Inge works on a new felt wall hanging for a client, laying out the pieces before she starts felting.

RIGHT Inge painted the floor blue-green because she wanted a recognizable style. 'When I'm in my studio, I am me, myself and I,' explains Inge.

BELOW Inge is mindful of working with ample daylight. A roof window sits directly above the landing window letting light flood in.

Opposite

TOP LEFT Balls of wall are organized in colours and stored on open shelves so that they are easily on hand for new projects.

TOP CENTRE Inge has created this fun display from a vintage teapot and cups. She uses the top one as a little vase.

TOP RIGHT Inge puts together pieces ready for a new project. She loves how felting is always an experiment and unpredictable.

CENTRE LEFT The vintage furniture, handmade furnishings and smile-inducing surprises combine to make this space unique and special.

CENTRE Soft balls of bright felting wool are arranged in a vintage suitcase on the studio floor, both practical and beautiful.

CENTRE RIGHT A tray is filled with toys that Inge's son played with. She enjoys using them as unexpected elements in her work.

BOTTOM LEFT Inge arranges things on the floor. 'If I put all my stuff on the floor, sometimes a great idea arises!' she says.

BOTTOM CENTRE Inge has added hooks to the wooden beams and made clever storage for her washi tapes from old clothes hangers.

BOTTOM RIGHT A large metal basket makes great storage for rolls of colourful wrapping paper that Inge uses for creative projects.

Above

Inge's studio is so colourful. 'All the coloured stuff just happened. It wasn't planned. I think it makes me happy and there are a lot of possible combinations with all the colours,' Inge explains.

Retro chic

Making colours sing

Artist and designer Sarah Hamilton lives in a stylish Mid-Century Modern house in a leafy corner of South East London with her husband and son. The house is situated close to Dulwich Woods, where Sarah enjoys living in her country oasis amongst the bustling city. Sarah and her husband lovingly restored this house with a deep respect for the vision the architect originally had for it. 'Houses are very precious,' explains Sarah, 'and they are only yours for a period of time, so it is important to respect and love them.'

There is a Scandinavian feel throughout Sarah's home, which is also indicative of her work. Sarah's love for her home is clear in her careful attention to every detail. Her stylish but welcoming interiors have been carefully collected to complement the age and style of the house. Her love of colour, pattern and design can be seen throughout the house, with fun flashes of joyful colours on doors, bold graphic prints, patterned rugs and cushions.

The use of colour in the home is enhanced by its wonderfully light and airy quality, with large windows looking out over the tall trees. This light feels like it flows

THIS PAGE The window looks into the living room and pours light into the kitchen. One of Sarah's large pencil drawings hangs above the Mid-Century sideboard and is complemented by the bright orange chair and the strong blues in the pot and bowl and the poster. 'The bright and happy Hawaii poster is my favourite thing in the kitchen,' explains Sarah.

through the whole house. The design and layout of the house is interesting and unusual with the kitchen on the ground floor, the two bedrooms and bathroom in the basement and Sarah's studio and the large living room upstairs.

It is not surprising that Sarah has filled her home with colour, as it plays such a vital role in her work. 'Colour is incredibly important to me. I've got a hit-list of strong colours, all punctuated by the herbs and spices of neutrals,' explains Sarah, sitting on her cosy pink sofa. 'Colours are like a recipe and they all play an important part. I will test and test again to get the colour absolutely right.'

Sarah's fascinating home really inspires her; she is passionate about architecture and has a deep appreciation of how unique and special her house is. In addition to its design, its location and setting is central to both her life and her work. 'I couldn't live in the countryside, but I'm very obsessed with the natural world. The house fulfils the countryside in me but also the city that I could never give up.'

ABOVE The simple but beautifully designed kitchen 'was built by my friend Steve, which makes it extra special to me,' says Sarah. The grey cupboards are reminiscent of one of Sarah's designs, with the pops of colour found in the kitchenware and posters working like the carefully selected colours Sarah uses in her work.

'Colour is incredibly important to me. I've got a hit-list of strong colours, all punctuated by the herbs and spices of neutrals,' explains Sarah.

BELOW This hallway leads into the two bedrooms and bathroom. Sarah's passion for colour continues here. 'I love using colour in my home because it warms me up. It's my antidote to the British climate!' she explains with a smile.

RIGHT Sarah loves bringing back treasures from her travels. 'I found this in Krakow, Poland, in a little side street. I spotted an artist's open studio and inside was an old man selling these gorgeous birds made from wood and twigs.'

OPPOSITE The happy pink door opens into one end of the living room. Wallpaper from fellow South London designers 'Mini Moderns' was hung up here for a joint open studio event and is a reminder of Sarah's love for working with other makers.

Sarah's work is deeply connected to the natural, so living surrounded by trees and nature is perfect for her. When this is combined with her city location, with its galleries, theatres and museums, you can understand why she loves her little corner of London so much.

It is clear that Sarah adores her home and is very settled in it, but travel is also a huge source of inspiration for her work. Globes, travel posters and trinkets from far-off lands fill her home. 'If I'm not travelling, I'm thinking about travelling,' she says dreamily. She loves looking at different places and finds it incredibly stimulating for her work. Years ago, Sarah saw Frida Kahlo's house in a book 'and I booked to go to Mexico within a

THIS PAGE Pretty leaf-patterned wallpaper works well with spots on the bedding and stripes on the rug in this master bedroom. Another travel poster, this time for India, fills Sarah's dreams, while a little bird, so often seen in Sarah's work, perches on the chest.

week,' she laughs. The colours, objects in her home and the imagery of Mexico came into her design work a lot and she still draws inspiration from the trinkets she brought back from her trip.

Sarah uses a distinctive colour palette and strives to 'make my colours sing'. Her designs are fresh and contemporary with a Mid-Century Modern and Scandinavian feel. 'Drawing is key to my work,' says Sarah. 'It is so important for creating a personal description of a shape and for mark-making. Computer-generated images don't achieve this. Drawing enables you to express your own visual language and is key to design, and to being distinctive.'

Designing and making in the UK is really important to Sarah and she is committed to producing all her work nationally. 'Made in the UK really matters to me,' she explains. 'Taking the decision to use only UK manufacturers makes it harder and more expensive, but it is really important to me.' Sarah is also a big champion of other UK makers and is a features writer for the magazine *ukhandmade*. She loves using social media to connect with other designer/makers. Sarah doesn't find it a competitive environment, indeed quite the opposite. 'It's such a wonderful community,' says Sarah, 'and I love the way everyone can support each other.'

ABOVE LEFT These beautiful vintage drawers were a special buy. 'I'd wanted one for a while, but they are hard to find. I was lucky to find this one. I love old shop fittings like this with all the drawers.'

ABOVE RIGHT This outdoor space leads out of the kitchen, creating a welcoming seating area for the warmer months. Sarah's colour palette extends out here too with the outdoor lights, deckchair and cute birdhouses.

THIS PAGE This cosy but stylish nook is beautifully conceived with the vintage seat and radio creating an inviting spot to take a rest. The calming blues on the carpet, wallpaper and seat all come together to make a real feature of this small space.

Natural inspiration

Sarah has a beautiful, bright, small studio in her home. The room is painted white, with white floorboards and large windows. 'A clean, pristine white space is really important for me to really extend my visual vocabulary of colour,' explains Sarah. The space is very organized, with a place for everything. Trinkets, vintage tins, pebbles and pretty shells provide inspiration for her drawings and designs, which she creates from a lovely vintage desk overlooking the trees. 'Being a maker is my entire life. Apart from my family, I don't love anything more in the world,' she says.

ABOVE LEFT Sarah stands at her drawing desk, looking through her large collection of sketchbooks for inspiration for new designs. Drawing is the foundation of all of Sarah's work.

ABOVE In Sarah's studio there is a display area where she brings together her current work in one place, from her colourful cards, her new bright trays and her collectable woodblocks.

Above

Sarah's bright, white studio, like the rest of the house, is full of natural light. This space is kept neat and organized to allow Sarah to concentrate on the details and colours of her work.

Opposite

TOP LEFT Colourful paper, drawings and cards fill this little corner, all on hand to help fuel new ideas and colour combinations.

TOP CENTRE Her drawing table looks out onto the trees, providing Sarah with great inspiration from the colours in the natural world.

TOP RIGHT Another little shelf of inspiration for Sarah's work. Tiny stones and sea urchin shells collected at the beach cluster together.

CENTRE LEFT Sarah collects treasures from all her travels to inspire her work. These quirky dolls are from her trip to Mexico.

CENTRE A screen printing frames sits in a corner. It shows how carefully Sarah combines colours to create her designs.

CENTRE RIGHT Sarah's sketches are pinned to her noticeboard, while one of her colourful Mexican toys hangs in front of them.

BOTTOM LEFT A bright green miniature toy sits on the windowsill, illustrating both Sarah's love of colour and her sense of fun.

BOTTOM CENTRE Sarah's collection now includes beautiful china mugs in her recognizable colours, which are made in the UK.

BOTTOM RIGHT Pencil drawings form an important part of Sarah's design process and she has a large collection of wonderful sketchbooks.

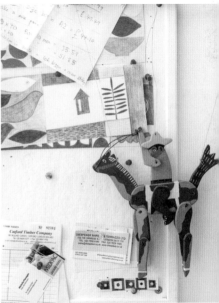

Light and bright

Textile designer Anna Joyce lives with her husband Victor and their two children in a beautifully styled, bright, Mid-Century Modern ranch-style house in Portland, Oregon. The house has huge windows and is high up, giving you a sense of being perched right up in the trees.

RIGHT The large windows on both sides of this living room bring in so much wonderful natural light, with green plants providing a lovely reflection of the trees outside. Anna's own designs on the cushions coordinate perfectly with her husband's artwork on the wall.

Anna moved to Portland with her husband after college and they have lived and worked in this house for eight years. Together they have created an inspiring, colourful home for their family. There is no doubt when you walk around this house that this is a maker home. The walls and shelves are full of their art, their children's art and Anna's parents' art.

Creativity and making are clearly right at the heart of this family and their home.

The interior is full of lush green plants, Mid-Century Modern furniture, books and colour; it is a cosy, welcoming place, full of character. The living space is open plan, which gives it a lovely feeling of family. 'My favourite thing about my home is the family art that

surrounds me,' Anna says with a smile. This house may be a small one, but it is a wonderfully inspirational example of how to create a stylish, family home even when space is limited.

Anna grew up in a creative family. 'As a child, I spent a lot of time in my mother's printing studio and my father's photography studio,' Anna explains,

LEFT The bright red shelves and table bring happy pops of colour to this side of the open-plan room. The children's wooden dolls' house sits alongside an area of the home devoted to the memory of Anna's father, who was also an artist.

ABOVE Anna loves listening to her father's record collection – her daughters especially love The Beatles and Stevie Wonder. Anna's dad passed away before her children were born, 'so listening to his music is a way for our entire family to be close to him,' she says.

'I feel comfortable, creative and powerful in this space,' explains Anna, thoughtfully.

pointing to an adorable photograph of her as a baby in a sling on her mother's back while she is working in her printing studio. Her parents also set up a gallery run by artists, where Anna was surrounded by more creative people and immersed in art.

At college, Anna studied print-making and later taught herself to sew after being given a sewing machine as a wedding gift. About five years ago she started her business, Anna Joyce Designs, by cleverly pulling together her print-making background with her newfound love of textiles.

Anna's home has a real influence on her work and is very special to her. 'I feel comfortable, creative and powerful in this space,' explains Anna, thoughtfully. She loves the light and looking out at the trees. As they change with the seasons,

ABOVE There is a strong sense of family in this home. 'These chairs are Wassily chairs that my father had in his photography studio. They add a lot of style to any room – they are one of my most treasured possessions,' Anna says.

LEFT The soda bottle is a porcelain sculpture that Anna's husband, Victor, made. The little mask sculptures are Mexican wrestling masks that Victor makes with the children whenever they play with clay. 'We have quite a collection of them now!' Anna explains, laughing.

BELOW The master bedroom is a family gallery with artworks by all the family members hanging as a collection. It is such a wonderful idea for displaying everyone's work whatever their age, and it is a lovely way to bring a family together. On the bed, different patterns and colours are combined to add further interest to this creative space.

ABOVE This wall has been painted teal to create both a calming and creative effect. It also makes the room appear a little darker than the rest of house, giving it a cosy feel. The wall is used to display one of Anna's husband's projects.

OPPOSITE TOP Anna made this lovely appliqué image of a deer family. 'When I was pregnant with our second child, I wanted to make something special. The image felt fun and stylish, but still expressed the maternal love I was feeling for the baby.'

OPPOSITE BOTTOM This beautiful cupboard in the girls' bedroom was painted for her eldest daughter by Anna's mother; a family treasure that will no doubt be kept in the family for generations to come.

they influence her work and her colour palettes. The spring blossoms, the bright summer greens, the reds and oranges of autumn and the browns of winter are a beautiful changing scene right in front of Anna's home. 'I love watching it rain from the windows too,' says Anna, who is clearly so connected to the nature that surrounds her home.

Anna loves living and working in Portland, especially because it is a very special place for makers. 'There is so much creativity here and makers are really supportive of each other,' says Anna. She explains that there is a healthy competition and makers push each other to get better. 'It is definitely one of the places that is experiencing a real renaissance in making, and you can still afford to make and live here,' explains Anna. All of Anna's work is sourced locally, her printer is local and it is also produced nearby. 'I can work really closely with my suppliers, which is a really important benefit to working in Portland,' she says. However, in contrast to the real sense of community Anna enjoys in Portland, she is sincerely grateful for and excited by the role that social media and the internet have played in building her business across the USA and the world.

> 'Portland is definitely one of the places that is experiencing a real renaissance in making and you can still afford to make and live here.'

Instagram, in particular, has enabled her to reach a much wider audience, and Etsy, the online marketplace for makers, artists and designers, has been really supportive of her work. I can connect with people and engage them in my work,' explains Anna. 'I often post an image of a new product or design idea on Instagram and, depending on the reactions people have, I know if I'm going in the right direction or need to go back to think again.'

The fabric of life

Anna's home studio sits in an inspiring corner of her home next to a large window. It may be tiny but it is perfectly formed and very beautiful. Plants hang from the ceiling and sit on her table, showing how much her work is connected to nature. Her family agreed to let her take over their dining table for her work, highlighting the value of making and art in her family. Anna started her business five years ago and has combined her history of print-making with her love of textiles to create wonderful ranges of homewares, bags and purses with her unique patterns and brilliant colours.

Above

TOP LEFT Here, Anna sits at her studio table painting new pattern ideas illuminated by the wonderful natural light from the windows surrounding her. It is a calm and inspiring place to work.
ABOVE LEFT Old jam jars and vintage mugs make great vessels for neatly holding Anna's supply of brushes. In such a small interior, it is important to have a place for everything.
ABOVE CENTRE Anna is particularly attached to her father's chairs. She is also very fond of their clean Mid-Century lines.

ABOVE RIGHT Piles of Anna's hand-painted and screen-printed, brightly coloured napkins and purses sit on the table.

Opposite

Anna loves that her studio is in the heart of our home. 'My girls watch me make art and we are all together when I am working,' says Anna, beaming.

All in the detail

Artist and letterpress designer, Kimberly Austin lives with her husband in a 1910 farmhouse with the most incredible views over the beautiful city of San Francisco. The couple live high up in the top apartment of the block, which Kimberly affectionately describes as 'the tree house'.

THESE PAGES When you walk up the stairs that lead into Kimberly's apartment, this is the scene that greets you. A beautifully styled, calm, inspiring space with light pouring in through the large windows and the additional skylights. You want to explore all the treasures, like the assembly of pretty figurines (left), straight away.

THIS PAGE Kimberly has covered this gorgeous French vintage daybed with a pastel blue fabric and made a beautiful collection of cushions to match. You can imagine taking a good book and a cup of tea and curling up on here, looking out at the views across San Francisco.

ABOVE This sweet vintage desk has been painted in a delicate mint green shade and creates a simple little space in the corner of the room.

This home is adorable, stylish and full of joy. With huge windows and a beautiful open living area, this small apartment is meticulously designed and light-filled. Kimberly's attention to detail is apparent from the moment you walk in – every element has been carefully thought about and pieced together.

Attracted to this building for its balance of history and character, Kimberly has lived here since 1998 and feels very fortunate to have found such a precious place to live. 'Space to me is such a personal necessity,' she explains, 'and looking for a space is a very emotional process.' Her love of this place is evident in the care and attention she gives it, not just when you look at the

gorgeous way her space has been put together but also in the ways the apartment fills the senses with the smell of candles (which she has designed), sweet posies of flowers and freshly baked scones.

French antique furniture, traded for Kimberly's artwork with friends who own a French vintage store, suits the space perfectly and complements all her little vintage finds and treasures, and the sense of history connected to both this building and to Kimberly's work. 'My space is so much a part of me and my work is so much a part of me that I don't see a separation between the two.'

This home is a work of love and you can tell that this couple have really got to know

THIS PAGE The huge black and white images hanging on the wall were created by Kimberly when she worked with polaroid cameras and experimented with different printing techniques. In contrast to the scale of the images a row of tiny vintage treasures is lined up along the top of the cabinet. The table and chairs are beautiful French vintage finds.

THIS PAGE Kimberly put a lot of attention into the bathroom and kitchen, filling it with unique, vintage finds. 'The result is a space that feels original to the 1910 era, but also has a very clean and modern sensibility,' explains Kimberly.

防原子防化学防细菌挂图

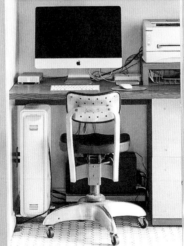

their space and grown with it. The way the apartment is laid out means that you can walk all the way around it in a circle – the whole space effortlessly flows from one room to the next. Every part fits together so beautifully. The time and effort they have put into finding every piece has certainly paid off to create this stylish, calm and comfortable space. When asked what her favourite piece is, Kimberly replies with a smile, 'Oh, the old French cabinet, which was originally used in an office. I love the colours and

BELOW The metal open shelving was sourced from a shop-fitting supplier. Filling it with white china and glassware creates a stylish look, especially when combined with the marble surfaces and white cabinets. The vintage stove completes the look.

RIGHT Like the main living room, the kitchen is also really bright. 'This room is filled with light and enough space to move around. We spend most of our time in the kitchen. It's a great gathering space,' enthuses Kimberly.

Both Kimberly's home and studio are painted white. 'Clean white space makes me feel happy. I feel like I am in a cloud or cotton ball. The light reflects off the white,' Kimberly explains.

BELOW This beautiful old French green chest is one of Kimberly's favourite antique pieces. The spaces left by the missing drawers have been put to good effect to display thoughtful mini collections from nature, travel and thrifting.

weathered paint, and all the drawers had little paper signs in to categorize them.'

Kimberly describes the importance of having 'a nurturing space that provides an environment to create things'. Her inspiration comes from old objects, camping trips, moss, pine cones on the ground, birdsong, old books and ephemera, embroidery patterns, reference books and antique pieces of jewellery. 'I have a respect for the past and a curiosity for how things work,' she says.

Kimberly has been a maker for as long as she can remember. 'As a young child, I always made things with whatever I could get hold of – it has always been a part of my nature,' she reminisces. At college she studied art, with a particular interest in photography. She spent time in Florence, Italy, studying art history, 'which filled my young mind with a passion for art and making things'. After college, Kimberly worked as a fine-art photographer with galleries for about 15 years before being tempted to try another medium. After buying a little letterpress, Kimberly started to change her studio bit by bit from photography to letterpress and the gorgeous Austin Press was born.

Kimberly beams with pride when she talks about the Maker

THIS PAGE The soft colour palette that Kimberly
has used to decorate her home continues into the
bedroom. A cute bedside table is delicately decorated
with a vintage telephone, fresh flowers, a tiny framed
picture, a seashell and a small vase, creating an image
of Kimberly's sources of inspiration.

LEFT Each piece in this vintage bathroom has been painstakingly sourced to create a gorgeous and soothing space. The tiny images mounted on wood are more of Kimberly's beautiful Polaroids. The honeycomb floor continues here, creating a harmonious flow from one room to the next.

ABOVE This cosy armchair with its sumptuous dark pink velvet cushion offers another lovely place to sit. The views across the city from this high-up apartment are breathtaking.

Movement. 'I feel so lucky that this is happening now because it's what I've always believed in,' she explains. Through her letterpress work, Kimberly has been able to create beautiful, small-scale products. She takes pride in making high-quality products that are meant to last and stay with you. 'People have been craving a connection with the things that we buy and use in our daily lives. We've grown so far away and detached from everything that we want to get back to this awareness of art, craft and quality. There are a lot of people putting their heart and soul into this. It's an exciting time,' Kimberly muses enthusiastically.

The stamp of authenticity

Kimberly's studio is in an old wooden warehouse building from the 1940s, situated on one of San Francisco's many docks. It is a simple structure, but much like her apartment, it is full of character and history. This connection to the past continues with her wonderful collection of letterpresses and vintage finds. Drawers and metal boxes of beautiful letterpress stationery are carefully organized and packaged. The whole space, with the old black machinery against the bright white ceilings and walls, is serene, calm and so inspiring.

BELOW Kimberly restored this large 19th-century letterpress herself. By taking it all apart, cleaning and fixing it, then putting it back together she learned how all the parts work.

BELOW RIGHT Behind the large wooden desk with yellow legs are rows of metal shelving and metal boxes filled with Austin Press stationery all ready to be shipped.

ABOVE Kimberly stands at one of her desks to put together a new order. All her products are handprinted in this studio and packaged by hand.

Above

TOP LEFT Kimberly pays careful attention to everything she designs and makes, including the way that she packages her products. Here she is wrapping a full set of letterpress alphabet cards by first tying them with twine.

TOP CENTRE Tiny pencils sit in a silver pot, next to a vintage cup of pens and scissors. Behind are the twine holders that Kimberly has fashioned, based on a 1910 design.

TOP RIGHT Everywhere you look in the Austin Press studio is another treasure. Here is a vintage paper crimper.

ABOVE LEFT Kimberly has designed these tiny little hand card holders, inspired by a Victorian design; perfect for her mini cards.

ABOVE CENTRE A pot of sepia ink lies on this wooden stool. 'The ink reminds me of the vintage photo processes I used in my darkroom,' Kimberly recalls wistfully.

ABOVE RIGHT A brand new printing plate has just arrived in the studio full of Kimberly's latest images. Her designs are inspired by rare books, vintage ephemera and small objects.

Opposite

Kimberly has painted all the walls and ceiling in her studio white. 'I can think clearly in white spaces. It creates a starting point from which you can go in any direction.'

Eclectic

Calm simplicity

Designer Erika Harberts lives in Rotterdam in the Netherlands with her husband and their two daughters in a 1980s house with a deceptively plain exterior and a delightfully surprising interior, bursting with inspiration, family life and creativity. Erika and her husband moved here 13 years ago when she was pregnant with her first daughter. They were attracted to the light flooding into the house, the big garden and its location really near to the centre of the city. 'You can cycle anywhere you want to go,' says Erika, 'and this area is lively but not too lively. It suits us perfectly.'

THIS PAGE Using these low lights over the dining table divides the space up in a simple and effective way. 'I enjoy crafting with the girls at the dining table; when it's full of craft materials, tea and treats, I think it's the heart of our home,' Erica says.

ABOVE This cabinet
was a gift from Erika's
grandparents. 'They used to
live in Morocco and brought
it back to Holland. It's filled
with little treasures from
them and ones we've
collected.' The painting
on the right is by Erika's
mother-in-law, depicting
St George, her husband's
family's saint.

This house is beautifully simple but with a real sense of style. 'I really try to be minimalist,' Erika says with a smile. 'When you have a smaller home, you have to live and work differently to make it work well. I often dream of bigger spaces, but I really enjoy living and working here.' White walls, wooden floors and the open-plan layout of the living areas all make the space feel larger than it is.

Although the house is a modest size, the family enjoy a beautiful garden where they have built a gorgeous *roulotte* (caravan), inspired by Erika's love of France. Erika

and her husband constructed this sweet little caravan as a playhouse for their girls when they were young and now it is a more sophisticated place for them to read, draw and relax in. Erika's studio is also situated in the garden, in a converted shed, so there is a strong connection between the home and the garden for this creative family.

Erika is greatly inspired by her two daughters. 'I really love creating with them and listening to them,' says Erika. 'It is such a great way to learn what they like and what they need. It really helps me to think of new products to make.' Erika's work is also deeply inspired by her love for Paris, travelling and visits to museums and galleries. 'I love to see art and sketch it, then come back home, influenced by what I've seen.'

When Erika was young, she dreamed of being a fashion designer and would spend hours sat at her grandmother's Singer sewing machine making dresses for her Barbie dolls. After finishing school, she studied fashion at college in Amsterdam, but it wasn't what she hoped it would be, so she left and took a year out to work in Paris, a city that has continued to be close to her heart and work ever since.

After she returned to the Netherlands, Erika went on to study free monumental art with textiles, which was followed by a job working in an art store. Shortly after her first baby was born, Erika started making little dolls and rabbits and blankets for her. She really enjoyed it and remembers getting great reactions to her work from friends and family. She then began to make things for friends and sold her products at little markets.

ABOVE Erika has created a sewing corner for her daughters at the end of the kitchen. 'The girls both use it to make bags, cushions and softies. They make them as presents for friends, to sell at craft markets or at school.'

FAR LEFT Although Erika's home is led by minimalism, she has put together several beautiful little collections, like this teal one on a kitchen shelf, which reflects the colour of the tiles.

LEFT Neatly arranged shelves above the girls' sewing station are filled with brightly coloured fabrics, sewing boxes, scissors and cute mini bunting. Erika puts a lot of effort into their shared love of making pretty things.

Erika's living room is calm and elegant with plenty of white space. On the sofa are two camera cushions made from fabric that she designed and printed for her daughter's camera-themed birthday party. Erika and her daughters enjoy planning themed parties together.

BELOW Erika has built up this pretty Russian doll collection over time. 'I love Russian dolls and somehow started a collection. Mostly I found them at second-hand markets, but some were gifts,' she explains.

ABOVE The pieces on this set of shelves are given plenty of room and white space, so they can all be appreciated fully. The ceramic goose was made by Erika's grandmother when she was about 75. It's from the story 'The Wonderful Adventures of Nils' by Selma Lagerlöf.

To begin with, Erika used pre-bought fabrics to make her dolls, but she had an ambition to create her own fabrics featuring her own designs, so she decided to learn about screen-printing fabric. After doing some reach online about fabric-printing courses and screen printing, she discovered blogs. Enchanted by what she found, she decided to start her own blog.

'I still remember my first blog post,' she says fondly. Shortly after Erika set up her Etsy store, people began to blog about her work as well. 'One of the first people to write about me was Irene Hoofs on her blog "Bloesem" and everything just evolved from there.'

At first, Erika printed everything herself, but now she is outsourcing her printing and

LEFT The girls' bedroom is bright and brimming with handmade loveliness. This cute reading nook is full of dolls that Erika has made. The tree and leaves painted on the wall give a storybook feel, and the curtains/drapes that close around the space make it extra cosy.

OPPOSITE LEFT As this room is quite small, Erika and her husband built most of it themselves, 'with some ready-made pieces like the beds that we altered. We kept the base white so that the girls could add their own details with posters, cushions and drawings.'

OPPOSITE RIGHT The girls both have desks in their bedrooms. Little stacks of washi tape, colourful pots of pens, pretty boxes, beautiful drawings and several collections of treasures all suggest that these girls are makers too.

she has started to outsource the doll making too, a clear sign that her business is growing.

Erika strongly believes that it would not be possible to be where she is now without social media and the internet, 'especially as a mother working from home'. Social media enables her to connect with other people and those who have the same interests but are maybe on the other side of the world. Erika has made great friends in the same way too, first developing friendships online and later in real life. 'I love to use social media like I would use a coffee machine in an office, where I can stop work for a few minutes to go and speak to people for some advice or just for some chit-chat.'

Erika also uses social media to enable her to develop her brand and new products. She likes

'I love to use social media like I would use a coffee machine in an office, where I can stop work for a few minutes to go and speak to people for some advice or just for some chit-chat.'

FAR RIGHT Erika's girls have developed their own drawing styles, which Erika supports by giving them the freedom to draw on black chalkboards around the house.

RIGHT Erika has recently redesigned the *roulotte* (caravan) 'to be more suitable for teenagers, with a sofa made from cushions that can be turned into a bed – easy for summer sleepovers,' explains Erika.

BELOW Erika and her husband designed and made the *roulotte* when the girls were little so that they could have a playhouse in the garden. The plants have grown up around it, creating a magical scene.

to take photographs of new sketches or ideas and share them on Instagram. 'It's a really great way to know if you're going in the right direction. You want people to be enthusiastic about your work, so it's ideal for judging this early on in the design process,' she explains.

Erika feels really privileged to do what she does. 'It has always been my dream to make my art into my life and work,' she stresses, but admits that it can be really hard to think commercially when you do something from your heart. 'You are driven by your creativity, your heart and your passion. The two biggest struggles are how to make money from this and how to be taken seriously by other people.' Erika goes on to explain how people think she is not really working if she is operating from home or doing something that they view as her hobby. But it is this that has driven her to be more successful and to 'get more acknowledgment that what I'm doing is a real job,' says Erika emphatically.

Available space

Erika and her husband converted their shed into her beautiful studio. With a true maker spirit, they fitted the insulation, painted everything, made all the cupboards from old kitchen cabinets and replaced the doors with wooden ones. Making and designing everything themselves means that it is all made to measure and perfect for the way Erika works. 'My desk is nice and long but not too deep. The mix of white and wood makes it feel fresh and creates a great base for my designs and materials,' explains Erika.

BELOW Erika has made a unique and charming shelving unit from a vintage dolls' house, which is perfect for a doll-maker's studio.

BELOW RIGHT Erika enjoys collecting mini vintage furniture and accessories. Here, a cute pink cabinet has a tiny sewing box on top. These inspire her accessory collections.

ABOVE Erika sits in her home studio making a new product. She has recently converted the garage into her studio, painting the whole space white to fill it with light.

Above

TOP LEFT Rolls of colourful twine and a sweet pair of scissors are all ready for Erika to wrap new orders.

TOP CENTRE Erika's dolls are inspired by her daughter Mila's seventh birthday party. 'After a trip to Paris, she wanted a Paris-inspired party with a Parisian outfit and a doll with a similar outfit', Erica recounts.

TOP RIGHT This miniature bicycle came from a shop that sells handmade items that have been made from recycled materials in developing countries.

ABOVE LEFT Like so many makers, Erika loves washi tape. She arranges it by colour in little collections around her studio.

ABOVE CENTRE Rolls of Erika's doll kits lean against a wall. Some get sewn together by Erika and some are sold as ready-to-sew kits.

ABOVE RIGHT Neat piles of Erika's cards and tags make it easy for her to pack orders. Her products always arrive beautifully wrapped.

Opposite

Erika and her husband have created a simple but inspiring space for her to work in. It has a similar feel to their home and is perfectly organized, tidy and as minimalist as a creative studio can be.

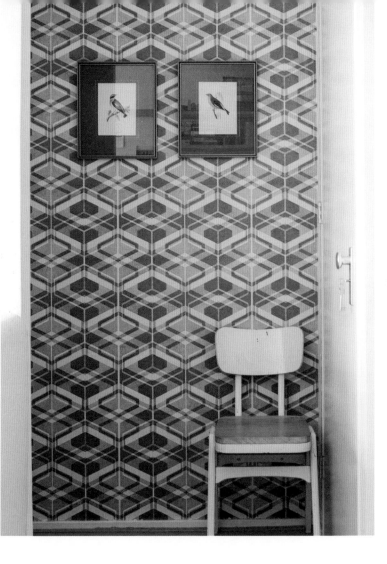

Still life

Illustrator Maartje van den Noort lives in a creative corner of Amsterdam in the Netherlands with her husband Ruben in a compact apartment built around 1900. Inside, the couple have created a simple, beautifully pared-back, calm and enchanting space, which encompasses their love of nature and the beach. Maartje's home is perfectly situated between the two places she works: her shared studio space towards the centre of Amsterdam and, in the opposite direction, the amazing co-working space she uses, which is packed full of traditional printing machines.

ABOVE Maartje made the vase cover when she worked at the shop Restored, where she sold her work along with other designers.

ABOVE CENTRE A beautiful tambourine sits next to this sweet oval-shaped bird picture – an example of the pared-back but beautiful look.

ABOVE RIGHT A large cactus sits on top of a storage box, creating a simple statement at the end of the room.

OPPOSITE The long, narrow open-plan apartment is divided up into the lounge, dining room and kitchen. The dining table was made by Ruben and is surrounded by six mismatched vintage chairs. The simple colours of the space are accented with occasional pops of bright colour.

When Maartje got married and first moved to Amsterdam to live with her husband four years ago, she had to seriously declutter and get rid of about 90 per cent of her things. 'I am such a collector and when I was single I had a big space all to myself. I am definitely a magpie, but I have loved the challenge of living with minimalism.' Not only have the couple had to bring their things together but also their different interior styles. You would never guess this though. The house exudes a feeling of effortless simplicity, with a nod to a beach- style vibe that comes from Ruben's love of the sea and surfing. Together they have created a quiet space but with a faint noise of creative collecting, with its piles of books, small collections of treasures and prints.

The apartment sits within their church community building and the couple played a part in choosing people to live in the other apartments. 'We all have our own homes, but we are all connected to the church,' explains Maartje. 'I love living close to our neighbours and they are all people who we know. It is a really great feeling.' Maartje enjoys living in this area of Amsterdam. 'It is a neighbourhood that is really developing and a lot of young families are moving here. There is a lovely community and village feel.'

To maximize the light in this narrow little space, the couple painted the wooden floors pale green and the walls white. They opted for open shelves in the living room rather than big white cupboards so that they could actually live with their possessions rather than hiding them away.

They have also made the most of their balcony and enjoy using it is an extra room, especially in the summer. 'I have

LEFT The kitchen cabinets are used as mini inspiration boards, with pictures and photographs held up with washi tape. The kitchen is small, so everything is carefully organized in the space. This baby blue coffee maker sits on top of the wooden bread bin, creating an eye-catching but practical feature.

BELOW LEFT The couple have cleverly made use of all the space in their small apartment, including this tiny little corner. Here, they have put up a bright red wall cabinet to hold china and underneath it they have mounted a coffee grinder on top of a narrow shelf that is just big enough to hold their coffee canisters.

BELOW 'I enjoy our kitchen because it is connected to the living room. It is small but has all we need. My dream is to have a big, light, open kitchen with a very big wooden table, made by Ruben. And always have fresh tea and fresh flowers on it,' explains Maartje.

LEFT As the apartment is small, the couple have made great use of their outdoor space with a large table, bench and chairs. The balcony is a good size and set high among the trees, which gives an instant connection to nature that so inspires Maartje's work.

BELOW 'I do change the little vignettes in our home, especially when I find something new, or open a box and rediscover old treasures. It's difficult to choose between all the little details, being the magpie that I am!' Maartje says.

One of my teachers told me to do fine art.' It was always clear that Maartje wanted to make, so she did go on to study fine art, but she didn't feel that was quite the right thing either. 'I wanted to make images without having to talk about them.' Eventually, Maartje began to draw again. 'I finally felt unstuck. Drawing is really my thing. It's what comes easy to me and what I love to do. I realised this is what I have to focus on.'

created a small garden with pots of plants,' Maartje says, 'and I enjoy coming and sitting out here and being inspired by nature and the outdoors.' Maartje's other influences include walks in the park and around the city, visiting art galleries and browsing Pinterest. 'I think influences build up in your mind. They stay there and accumulate until the right moment comes to remember them again,' explains Maartje. 'I love to capture moments, like watching a bird for example. I want to capture it, keep it and make it mine. Drawing enables me to do that. It enables me to translate all these influences from nature, from conversations, from other artists, and to connect it to my own imagery.'

Maartje has been making and drawing since she was a child, but it took her quite a while to realise that she could actually make a career from it. After school she studied graphic design in Rotterdam, 'but I wasn't tidy enough. I was messy and couldn't finish off the fine details that graphic design requires,' she says with a smile. 'It was a good creative time and a good time for developing my style, but I was never going to be a graphic designer.

Drawing room

Today, Maartje loves working in Amsterdam with its creative networks and the city's openness to new things and ideas. She has a lovely studio with great natural light in an old building, which she shares with friends. 'I really enjoy sharing a studio and having people around me to have lunch with and be inspired by.' Maartje also works in a co-working space with a difference. It is a 'graphic work space' full of vintage letterpress machines, other beautiful printing presses and drawers and shelves of equipment. It is like a wonderful museum but one that Maartje feels fortunate enough to work in.

OPPOSITE TOP LEFT The natural tones of Maartje's work are punctuated by pops of bright colour. A scarf that she made hangs on the mannequin and a bird mobile floats from the ceiling.

OPPOSITE TOP RIGHT Maartje's delicate sketches on loose sheets are bound together with ribbon. The shades of paper she uses, particularly the greys and browns, give a very natural, gentle feel to her work.

OPPOSITE BOTTOM LEFT Maartje sits at her drawing desk next to a large window, working on some new sketches. She divides her time between working here and at the graphic co-working space.

THIS PAGE 'This is where I collect work of my own and little finds that inspire me. This helps me get a grip on the style and atmosphere that I like to create with my work,' Maartje explains.

OPPOSITE If there is one thing you can say about makers, it is that they're inventive. Every inch of this fascinating home is used for either function or display – sometimes both! So much of the space is handmade or adapted in some way – something that epitomizes the makers' DIY aesthetic.

LEFT There is something about Mid-Century design that appeals to the modern-day maker. Timeless design pieces like this desk make for a beautiful home work environment that supports creative clutter being something to celebrate, not to hide away in a cupboard.

Full colour

Illustrator and educator Kate Bingaman-Burt lives in a small but perfectly formed apartment building in Portland, Oregon, with her husband Clifton and their dog Mabel. The couple have lived here since the summer of 2008 when they moved to Portland from Mississippi. For the first two years, Kate also worked in the apartment, until her husband confessed that, 'I feel like I'm living in your brain. We need to find you a space outside of the apartment!' This was a decision that, Kate admits, proved to be good for both her health and mental wellbeing.

ABOVE The small kitchen is beautifully designed and has open shelves that add to the open feeling of the whole apartment. 'We did zero to the kitchen. The awesome architect Kevin Cavenaugh did it all,' explains Kate.

LEFT 'These guitars belong to Clifton and he plays them all. I can play a very sad and soulful rendition of 'Blister in the Sun' by The Violent Femmes and that is about it', Kate admits.

Kate's apartment is bursting with life and colour. The walls are busy with images and words and there is inspiration to soak up wherever you turn. The open-plan space has a really high ceiling, making it feel more spacious than it really is, and it creates a unique and interesting space. When you walk into the interior, the character, style and taste of Kate and her husband shout a big, welcoming 'hello!'

Living in a small space has really helped Kate to think about her possessions and to keep a regular check on the things she has gathered. 'I call myself a maximalist, while my husband is most definitely a minimalist,' Kate says with a smile. She creates layers of things that she is inspired by and combines this with colours that she likes. Her home and studio are her big inspiration places. 'I am a real homebuddy, probably the most introverted extrovert you'll ever meet. If I have the option, I would rather stay home than go out.' explains Kate. 'One of my favourite places in the world is behind my grandmother's drawing table with my headphones on,' Kate says happily. Her grandparents were both illustrators and her grandmother illustrated over a thousand children's books. 'She was always working and drawing from age 19 until she was in her mid-70s,' explains Kate. 'But she always had time to stop and talk and show me her pens and tools when I went down to her wonderful basement studio.' When her grandmother passed away a couple of years ago, Kate inherited her drawing table and it is clearly such a precious thing to her. 'I never felt like I could draw and I didn't start illustrating until eight or nine years ago. I never thought I'd be able to share the same career as my grandmother, but I feel stupidly lucky to be able to do that,' says Kate

THIS PAGE The walls in this home are busy, yet they are full of interesting images and design. Filling a small apartment with so much could feel cluttered, but Kate has created a space that feels energetic but balanced. It makes you want to stop, look and be inspired.

THESE PAGES The huge metal frame windows give this apartment an industrial feel. Kate and Clifton have filled the space with colour. 'Colour makes me feel GOOD! Without it... sad times.' The white shelves opposite were designed by Clifton and built by one of Kate's students when they both lived in Mississippi. 'We love them and want to make more!'

reflectively. Today, drawing is everything to her: 'I can tell during the school year when I've been teaching too much and not had enough drawing time, I get so cranky.'

Kate has been influenced by the illustrator Saul Steinberg for a long time. When she was growing up, her aunt and uncle lived in New York City and always had his books lying around. 'I just loved, and still do, his lines, humour and also sometimes his seriousness. The simple complexity of his work has always blown me away.' Kate is also inspired and influenced by design that doesn't look like it has been designed, such as forms, receipts and bits of paper. 'I can spend hours in office supply stores and antiques shops. I love objects and the history of objects,' explains Kate. 'I even met my husband at his yard sale!'

When Kate was at university, she studied art minor classes alongside her English major, including a graphic design class led by a graphic design professor who changed the way she thought about graphic design. 'He just blew my mind with what graphic design could be. It was a big tipping point for me to discover it wasn't just all about logos,' she explains. After finishing her studies, Kate worked as a designer for a gift company, where she became fascinated by the things people buy and sell. She began to fill notebooks with observations about consumption and became really interested in why we consume. She took this further at graduate school and started her project 'Obsessive Consumption' where she photographed everything she bought for 28 months and uploaded it to a website. The project that followed was her Daily Drawings, which initially started as a way of punishing herself for getting into credit card debt, but ended up as a way for her to clear her debts, fall in love with drawing and become an illustrator. Art directors saw her work online and commissioned her, and people wanted to buy her drawings and illustrations. 'It was a weird cyclical thing,' explains Kate, 'and I really enjoy the collaborations and opportunities that have come from my drawings. I love being an illustrator!'

ABOVE Kate and her husband were really attracted to the architecture of this building, particularly the high ceilings. 'We LOVE this about the space. It makes a small area feel huge!'

RIGHT 'This vase was made by Scott Barry and I bought it when we first moved to Portland. It's one of my favourite things,' Kate explains.

OPPOSITE 'I like to mix a little bit of my stuff with a lot of other people's work. I'd love to change our artworks frequently. I have a huge file filled will unframed prints. A goal is to one day spend a few days just framing them.'

FAR RIGHT Why should your bookshelf be ordered alphabetically or by any other way than by the colour of the spine? Makers like Kate love these details.

THESE PAGES Kate shares her studio, so she just has a corner of the room. However, she has filled this space with colour and fun. A gigantic pretzel hangs from the ceiling, while a pair of large eyes sits watchfully on the windowsill.

ABOVE Kate sits at her precious drawing desk that she inherited from her grandmother and draws in one of her many sketchbooks. It is perhaps her happiest place to be.

Open and ink

Kate works in a shared studio in an old Ford factory of the early 1900s. The famous Model T was built here and rumour has it that the elevator was designed to hold the vehicle, as they would take it up to the roof for the paintwork to dry! Kate clearly loves the history and stories attached to the building. She shares her space with four others, including her husband, all of whom are illustrators and designers. 'There's a really nice working vibe here,' says Kate, 'and it's so much better to be here than working from home.'

Opposite

TOP LEFT These pictures are from Kate's eight-year drawing project. From 2006–14, she drew something she purchased every day.

TOP CENTRE Kate's studio wall is busy and full of inspiration. 'I add and edit, and sometimes I rip it all down and start over again.'

TOP RIGHT Like her home, Kate's studio is bright and colourful. 'My studio is about 95% other people's stuff and 5% of mine.'

CENTRE LEFT Kate loves to make zines with her illustration work and she often gives them out instead of business cards.

CENTRE Another image from Kate's daily consumption project. 'I love documenting objects that we engage with everyday,' she explains.

CENTRE RIGHT 'In 2015, I'm starting a project with a monthly drawing project, with the end result manifesting in a zine.'

BOTTOM LEFT Every surface can become a scrapbook – a place to stick a reminder of something you find interesting, beautiful or inspiring.

BOTTOM CENTRE Kate has created a great set of colourful storage for her pens and other stationery with these mini red buckets.

BOTTOM RIGHT One of Kate's drawings of a book by Saul Steinberg, who has been a big influence on her for a long time.

Above

Kate's personality is written large here. Every surface reveals a part of her character and there are echoes of her work in every detail.

Making a living

For all the makers featured in this book, making is their profession and, in an increasingly competitive world they need to ensure that they work hard at promoting their products and services. When you do something you love and your art is so much a part of who you are, it can often be difficult to place a value on the things you produce. Here the makers featured in the book give their tips for turning a hobby or passion into a successful business.

Alix Blüh

'In truth, I was one of those lucky people who always knew what they wanted to do in life. It was more of a driving need, an obsession perhaps, than a want.

Fortunately I had very supportive parents who exposed me to art and provided me with the opportunities to learn craft. I remember being particularly inspired by the silversmith's studio in the summer camp that I went to aged 12. I spent every possible moment in there, fascinated by what I could make. It was then that I knew that I wanted to be a jeweller.

It was with the prompting of a friend at age 18 that I starting selling to a local gallery. In those early years, I made my contacts with stores by simply walking in. This was long before the age of internet, so everything was done in person or by phone. What really transformed my career making the decision to move to San Francisco in 1992. That is where I tackled the long time desire to be a metalsmith, but I stayed true to my original concepts with a strong passion for reliquaries and homages to antiquity. My career grew exponentially after I started attending the New York City wholesale trade shows, and I then had to hire a full-time bench jeweller.

My advice is to start by truly understanding who your audience is. If you know who you are designing for, half the battle is won. The wonderful thing about launching a business today is that you have access to countless resources, guides and mentors online. Marketing in the digital age is tremendously multi-dimensional, and social media platforms can really help to boost your visibility.'

Anna Joyce

'I spent a month cleaning, organizing and preparing my studio before going full time. I knew I needed my work space to be ready to handle whatever was thrown at it. I developed a logo, and set about branding my shop. All of these preparations took place before I started working on my business full time. I wanted to make sure I was ready to work in a professional way.

Invest in professional photography and styling that really makes your work shine. Today, when so much selling and marketing takes place online, your best tool is great images. Professional photography also makes it easy for magazines and blogs to feature your work. It is by far the best investment I make in my business every season.'

Donna Wilson

'When I first started out I had no idea that it would lead to employing people. As for my dream becoming a business, I think I'd always thought that I'd be knitting away alone in my basement! For me it's been such an organic process, and everything's happened in stages, so I almost don't notice. I really believe in hard work, and I used to work every hour of the day, sometimes knitting or sewing on the bus on the way to a meeting. I said YES to every opportunity that came my way. I think it's important to be open to different things, as you never know where they might lead.

I always tell people to be unique – find your own voice and style and stick to your principles. It's a very competitive world so you need to stand out from the crowd.'

Erika Harberts

'After art school, I started working in a shop and didn't know how to earn my living through my creative work. But when my girls where born I was home a lot more and started to make things for them. At the same time I learned about blogs and Etsy and did some craft markets. I realized that my heart was in creating and designing products instead of art. I started blogging and selling through Etsy and gradually my business started to grow.

Follow your heart and instinct. Believe in yourself and don't be afraid to think big(ger). My business started to grow after I dared to make some bigger decisions like outsourcing labour, so I could focus on other parts of my work.'

Inge Cremer

'When I was young, I was always creating handmade things for my bedroom. I loved changing things around and styling it. I really knew I wanted to work in a creative job, so after school I went on to study styling and decorating at college. I went on to do lots of different jobs and gain plenty of experience. It really helped me to get to know what I liked and didn't like. Gradually I built up my own business, at first taking on all requests until I was in a position to pick and choose. My advice is to gain experience and knowledge, be motivated and patient, but the most important thing is to follow your heart and be yourself!'

Kate Bingaman-Burt

'It began when I started getting enquiries for freelance work after a few months of sharing my Daily Purchase drawing project. I just started saying yes to everything, and I feel like I have been playing catch up ever since. Repetition is a pretty powerful thing and when combined with consistently sharing work online (and in person), you identify yourself as someone who does that thing. The way that my drawing

project transformed into a business was by a cycle of drawing, posting and sharing online, and then saying yes to some opportunities that initially really scared me.

I am still pretty uncertain with a lot of business things. I think that seeking out a mentor (or two or three), who is working in a way that you want to be working and then learning from them, is a great place to start.'

Kimberly Austin

'Ever since I was a kid, I have always made things. If all I had was macaroni, construction paper, and elmer's glue, then they would be my coveted art materials for the day. There has never been a transition for me, just an evolution. The evolution from

hobby to profession is simply a product of a lifetime of using my hands and imagination, combined with my burning desire to make beautiful things.

I believe in passion and commitment. Turning something you love to do into your profession is not a small task. Lots of hard work and perseverance are behind the scenes. All those pieces fit together like a puzzle, and the puzzle is a journey. Embrace all the surprises and learning experiences to shape your business into something that is uniquely you.'

Maartje van de Noort

'I was always passionate about doing something creative, and after getting through my education and art

school, I knew that creating, drawing and making images was what I wanted. After initial long struggles with fine art, I learned to accept that it wasn't for not me, and that what I love most – drawing and designing – should be my thing. Of course, it did not pay from the start, but eventually it grew to be my way of creating income, while at the same time, making me feel like I was following my gut.

Dream and go for the big picture, but take your time and learn to understand and respect your limits. If you need to stop and move in a different creative direction, then don't be afraid to do that.'

Sarah Hamilton

'Becoming an artist/designer was always my ambition, so I began my business immediately after leaving college. I identified a few dream shops I wanted to work with and sent them examples of my designs, which, fortunately, they loved. This gave me the confidence and funds to develop further work, so I could grow my business by building on the initial successes.

Think of social media as your very best friend. As a small business it's a fantastic way to interact with other businesses, meet clients, locate suppliers and access support and

advice. Great product photography is money well spent. Images are the gateway to getting your designs seen and ultimately purchased. Be open-minded and create opportunities with others – collaboration is a great way to build your business and mutually support others.'

Sarah Owen

'Art and design have sustained me literally and figuratively along a pretty smooth path from passion to profession. I've always experimented with my own interiors and transformed each space I've lived and/or worked in. Opening the doors and sharing my passion with my community, in person and online, has led to invitations to collaborate on one project after another.

Listen thoughtfully to what your clients say about how they will use their space, what they love about it, what challenges it poses. Once you have an understanding of the personal priorities within the space, you can start to create the physical environment in that context. Interiors can be inspiring and therapeutic when the physical elements of the space support the lifestyles within it.

Teresa Robinson

'I started making jewellery when I was young, without any idea of what it would take to make a living out of it. I started small. I had about a dozen necklaces that I packed up into a cigar box, and took to a couple of local shops that I knew sold indie designers work on consignment.

A few pieces started to sell here and there, and so I got a website made, and took out an ad in a magazine, and things just kind of snowballed from there. I think I was very lucky in that I was making just the right thing, at just the right time, and it appealed to the right demographic. It was also back in the early 2000s, at sort of the genesis of the modern DIY and crafting movement, and Etsy wasn't even really a thing yet. So I had much less competition thank folks who are starting out now. This business is still a work in progress, and over 12 years in, I still feel like I'm learning as I go.

My advice is to do something you believe in, and work with integrity. Try to find your own voice, differentiating yourself from what others are doing. Dedicate time to work on your project every day, and be patient. If you're making from a place that's authentic, it's bound to pay off.'

Vicky Trainor

'There has never really been a transformation – it's been an organic journey. My passion for textiles and design has been there since I was young, and I studied fashion and textile design at university.

I love the freedom of moving between interiors, interior design, styling, stationery, fashion products, vintage sourcing, stationery and marketing. I'm not a fan of routine and this way of working suits me.

Be creative every day. Whether that's a few words in a notebook, a sketch or two, a walk in the park, a few hours lost in Pinterest – the list is endless. If you're passionate and love what you do it should shine through in the work you produce.'

Sources

WORLDWIDE

BRIKA
www.brika.com
A marketplace that celebrates
modern craft.

BRIT.CO
www.brit.co
Inspiration, lessons and marketplace
for the female DIY generation.

DIY.ORG
www.diy.org
Ideas to encourage your kids to be
mini makers.

ETSY
www.etsy.com
A marketplace and community
for makers.

FAB FOUNDATION
www.fabfoundation.org/fab-labs/
Maker spaces with 3D printers
and laser cutters.

FOLKSY
www.folksy.com
A global market place for
British craft.

GREAT.LY
www.great.ly
A marketplace for makers curated
by tastemakers.

IMAKR
www.imakr.com
Get into 3D printing with workshops
and kit.

INSTRUCTABLES
www.instructables.com
Videos to help you learn how to
make a number of surprising things.

MAKE
www.makezine.com
A magazine that celebrates making.

#MAKEITSEWCIAL
www.instagram.com/allison_sadler_
A weekly global celebration of
making and craft on Instagram.

MAKERBOT
www.makerbot.com
The affordable 3D printer that
started a movement.

MAKER FAIRE
www.makerfaire.com
Events to find out all about the
Maker Movement.

MAKERVERSITY
www.makerversity.co.uk
Learn all about how to make
with these courses.

MASTERED
www.mastered.com
Learn to master your craft with
online educational videos

PINTEREST
www.pinterest.com
Create and share inspiration boards.

PRODUCT HUNT
www.producthunt.com
Discover curated collections of
useful digital tools.

RAVELRY
www.ravelry.com
A community site and resource
for knitting and crochet.

THINGYVERSE
www.thingiverse.com
A network of 3D designers sharing
their work.

WEWORK
www.wework.com
A network of beautiful co-working
spaces, and useful articles.

UK

COCKPIT ARTS
www.cockpitarts.com
A space for makers in London
that's home to so many great
small companies.

THE CRAFTS COUNCIL
www.craftscouncil.org.uk/
Supporting UK craft and the trade
body for craftspeople.

CRAFTY FOX MARKET
www.craftyfoxmarket.co.uk
A regular event all about makers
sharing their work.

THE MAKERSCAFE
www.makerscafe.com
A drop-in lasercutting and 3D
printing shop for the coffee lover.

THE MAKERY
www.themakery.co.uk
Craft and sewing workshops.

MOLLIE MAKES
www.molliemakes.com/
Monthly magazine for inspirational
projects to do at home.

RAZORLAB
www.razorlab.co.uk/
Get something cut out of almost
any material via laser cutter.

SHAPEWAYS
www.shapeways.com/
Upload your 3D design and have it
printed out of a variety of materials.

SMUG
www.ifeelsmug.com/products/work
shops
Classes and creative business
workshops.

THE TRAMPERY, LONDON
www.thetrampery.com
Kitch and retro co-working spaces
in London that have a homely feel.

US

ADX PORTLAND
www.adxportland.com
A hub for collaboration where
individuals come to learn and make.

BROOKLYN MAKERS
www.brooklynmakers.com
Unique and handmade goods
made in Brooklyn.

INDY HALL
www.indyhall.org
One of the original maker spaces,
Alex Hillman helped spawn a
movement.

THE MAKER CO-OP, AUSTIN
www.themakercoop.com
A group of individual makers
in Austin.

MAKE:SF
www.meetup.com/makesf
San Francisco maker community.

THE MAKESHIFT SOCIETY
www.makeshiftsociety.com
Beautiful co-working spaces in
San Francisco and Brooklyn.

**MARTHA STEWART
AMERICAN MADE**
www.marthastewart.com/american
made/shop
Support for and celebration of
American makers.

PORTLAND MADE
www.portlandmade.com
A self-sustaining community of
makers, artisans and manufacturers.

RE:MAKE
www.remake.brit.co
Conference all about gathering
makers together.

RENEGADE CRAFT FAIR
www.renegadecraft.com
Network of events celebrating
the DIY craft movement.

EUROPE

BETAHAUS BERLIN
www.betahaus.com/berlin/
Inspiring Berlin maker space.

DESIGNTORGET
www.designtorget.se/designtorget/se
All the best Swedish design in one
place.

**GRAFISCH WERKCENTRUM,
AMSTERDAM**
www.grafischwerkcentrumamsterda
m.nl
A co-working space that celebrates
traditional printing techniques.

THE MAKERS AMSTERDAM
www.themakersamsterdam.com
A project to uncover and portray
the makers of Amsterdam.

MAKERS MARKET BERLIN
www.makersmarket.de
A large craft market supporting
local makers in Berlin.

RDM MAKER SPACE
www.rdmmakerspace.nl
Inspiring space for makers
in Rotterdam.

**THE THINKING HUT,
AMSTERDAM**
www.thethinkinghut.com
Creative co-working space
in Amsterdam.

Picture credits

Endpapers The home and studio of designer/maker Vicky Trainor of The Linen Garden, North Yorkshire, England; **1** Artist and designer Sarah E. Owen; **2–4** The home and studio of the artist/stylist Inge Cremer in the Netherlands; **5** Illustrator and artist Maartje van den Noort www.maartjevandennoort.nl; **6–9** The home of photographer/maker Emily Quinton and artist/technologist Stef Lewandowski; **10–11** MakersCafe in Shoreditch, London www.makerscafe.com; **12 above left and below left** MakersCafe in Shoreditch, London www.makerscafe.com; **12 right–15** Illustrator/artist Maartje van den Noort www.maartjevandennoort.nl; **16** The home and studio of jeweller Alix Blüh and photographer Michael Jang in San Francisco; **17 above** Teresa Robinson; **17 centre** The home and studio of jeweller Alix Blüh and photographer Michael Jang in San Francisco; **17 below** Artist and designer Sarah E. Owen; **18–29** Artist and designer Sarah E. Owen; **30–41** The home and studio of jeweller Alix Blüh and photographer Michael Jang in San Francisco; **42–53** Teresa Robinson; **54** The home and studio of the artist/stylist Inge Cremer in the Netherlands; **55 above** The home and studio of textile and product designer Donna Wilson in London; **55 centre** The home and studio of designer/maker Vicky Trainor of The Linen Garden, North Yorkshire, England; **55 below** The home and studio of the artist/stylist Inge Cremer in the Netherlands; **56–67 above** The home and studio of textile and product designer Donna Wilson in London; **68–79** The home and studio of designer/maker Vicky Trainor of The Linen Garden, North Yorkshire, England; **80–91** The home and studio of the artist/stylist Inge Cremer in the Netherlands; **92–93 above** The home of designer and author Anna Joyce in Portland, Oregon; **93 centre** The home of the artist and designer Sarah Hamilton in London; **93 below** Kimberly Austin of Austin Press, San Francisco; **94–105** The home of the artist and designer Sarah Hamilton in London; **106–115** The home of designer and author Anna Joyce in Portland, Oregon; **116–127** Kimberly Austin of Austin Press, San Francisco; **128** The home of the illustrator Kate Bingaman-Burt in Portland, Oregon; **129 above** The home of the illustrator Kate Bingaman-Burt in Portland, Oregon; **129 centre** The home and studio of designer Erika Harberts of mikodesign from the Netherlands; **129 below** Illustrator and artist Maartje van den Noort www.maartjevandennoort.nl; **130–141** The home and studio of designer Erika Harberts of mikodesign from the Netherlands; **142–149 below** Illustrator and artist Maartje van den Noort www.maartjevandennoort.nl; **150–161** The home of the illustrator Kate Bingaman-Burt in Portland, Oregon; **163** The home of photographer/maker Emily Quinton and artist/technologist Stef Lewandowski; **164** Teresa Robinson; **165** The home and studio of the artist/stylist Inge Cremer in the Netherlands; **166–167** The home and studio of jeweller Alix Blüh and photographer Michael Jang in San Francisco; **168** The home of designer and author Anna Joyce in Portland, Oregon; **169** Kimberly Austin of Austin Press, San Francisco; **170** The home and studio of jeweller Alix Blüh and photographer Michael Jang in San Francisco; **173** The home and studio of artist/stylist Inge Cremer in the Netherlands; **176** The home of maker/photographer Emily Quinton and artist/technologist Stef Lewandowski.

Business credits

ALIX BLÜH
www.alixbluh.com and

MICHAEL JANG
www.michaeljang.com
16, 17 centre, 30–41, 166–167, 170.

ANNA JOYCE
www.annajoycedesign.com
92, 93 above, 106–115, 168.

DONNA WILSON
+44 (0) 207 749 0768
info@donnawilson.com
www.donnawilson.com
55 above, 56–67.

EMILY QUINTON
http://Makelight.io and

STEF LEWANDOWSKI
http://Stef.io
6–9, 163, 176.

ERIKA HARBERTS
www.mikodesign.nl
129 centre, 130–141.

INGE CREMER
www.Ingevilt.nl
2–4, 54, 55 below, 80–91, 165, 173.

KATE BINGAMAN-BURT
www.katebingamanburt.com
128, 129 above, 150–161.

KIMBERLY AUSTIN
www.austinpress.com
93 below, 116–127, 169.

MAARTJE VAN DEN NOORT
www.maartjevandennoort.nl
and

SASKIA DE VALK
www.vlinderenvogel.com
and

**GRAFISCH
WERKCENTRUM AMSTERDAM**
www.grafischwerkcentrumamsterdam.nl
5, 12 right–15, 129 below, 142–149.

MAKERSCAFE
Old Shoreditch Station,
1 Kingsland Rd,
London E2 8DA
www.makerscafe.com
10–11, 12 above left, 12 below left.

SARAH HAMILTON
+44 (0) 208 299 6647
shlprints@aol.com
www.sarahhamiltonprints.com
93 centre, 94–105.

SARAH E. OWEN
Art + Interiors
www.saraheowen.com
1, 17 below, 18–29.

TERESA ROBINSON
Tiro Tiro
www.tirotiro.com
17 above, 42–53, 164.

VICKY TRAINOR
www.thelinengarden.co.uk
www.etsy.com/shop/vickytrainor
www.thelinengarden.blogspot.com
and

**FLOWERS BY
DARLING & GREEN**
www.darlingandgreen.co.uk
Endpapers, 55 centre, 68–79.

Index

Figures in *italics* indicate
captions.

A

Amsterdam 12–13, 142–9
Anna Joyce Designs 110
Anthropologie *70*
armchairs *124*
Arts and Crafts 71
artwork, displaying *112*
attic studios 88–91
Austin, Kimberly *40*, 116–27
Austin Press 122, *125–7*

B

balconies 144, 147, *147*
Barry, Scott *156*
baskets *90*
bathrooms
  homespun *64*, *75*
  retro chic *124*
  rustic *38*
bedrooms
  children's 62, *62–3*, *113*,
    136, *137*
  eclectic *136*, *137*
  homespun 62, *62–3*, *87*
  retro chic *112*, *113*, *123*
  rustic *24*, *36–7*, *49*
beds 23, *24*, 25
Bell, Vanessa 71, *75*
Bethnal Green, London 65
Bingaman-Burt, Kate 150–61
blogs and bloggers 14, 47, 87
  Bloesem blog (Irene Hoofs)
    134
Bloomsbury Group 71
Blüh, Alix 9, 13, 30–41
bottles, glass *28*
Brooklyn, New York City 10
bunting *77*, *78*, *133*
Burt, Clifton 151, 152, *152*,
  154–5, 155

C

cabinets *68*, *132*
caravan playhouse 132, *138*
Carlos, Debbie *48*
Cavenaugh, Kevin *152*
ceramics 37
chandeliers *84*
chest of drawers *74*
children's rooms
  eclectic *136*, *137*
  homespun 62, *62–3*
  retro chic *113*
china, displaying *68*, *121*
clothes, hanging *62*
co-working spaces 10–15, 18,
  148, 158–61
Cole and Son *47*
colour
  eclectic *145*
  retro chic 95, 97–8, *97*, *108*
  rustic *35*
Couverture 64
Craft Carriage *26*
crates, as shelving *18*, *66*
Cremer, Inge 80–91
cupboards
  eclectic *146*
  homespun *57*, *62*, *83*
  kitchen *62*, *146*
cushions *36*, *78*, *94–5*

D

'Daily Drawings'
  (Bingaman-Burt) 156
daybeds *88*, *118*
desks *118*, 151, *159*
dining areas
  eclectic *131*, *145*
  homespun *73*, *84*
  lighting *19*, *46*, *131*
  rustic style *19*, *21*, *46*
  tables *145*
displays
  china *121*
  cupboards *57*
  jewellery *40*
  vintage china *68*

dolls 134, 137, *140*
drawers, vintage *101*
drawing 101, *103*, *105*, 147,
  152

E

eBay *61*
eclectic 128–61
Enrichment core study 34
Ercol 59, *61*, *64*
Etsy 14, 47, 113, 134

F

fab labs 10
fabric
  floral *72*
  vintage *77*, *78*
Facebook 13–14
family homes 9, 108–15
felting 85, *86–9*
floral patterns and prints
  68–9, *72*
Ford factory 158–61
frames *28*, *83*
  as wall decorations *21*
French antique furniture 118,
  119, 121, *122*

G

galleries
  Alix Blüh *40*
  gallery walls *34*
garages, as studios 50–3
glass bottles *28*
Gorinchem 68–91
Grafisch Werkcentrum
  (Graphic Work Centre),
  Amsterdam 12
GREAT.LY 14

H

hackspaces 10
hallways *58*, 59, *98*
Hamilton, Sarah 94–105

Harberts, Erika 130–41
homespun 54–91
Hoofs, Irene 134

I

industrial spaces and style
  eclectic *154–5*, *156*
  rustic 16–29, *30–1*
inspiration boards *146*
Instagram 13–14, 113, 138
installations 22, *22*
Internet 13–14, 113, 137, 138

J

Jang, Michael 30–4, *38*
jewellery 36, 37
  displaying *40*
  Teresa Robinson 45, 50–3
Joyce, Anna 106–15

K

Kahlo, Frida 98
kitchens
  cupboards *62*, *146*
  eclectic *146*, *152*
  homespun *62*, *72*, *80*, *81*
  industrial style *20*
  injecting colour in *35*, *97*
  retro chic 97, *97*, *120*, *121*
  rustic *18*, *20*, *21*, *35*, *45*
  shelving *18*, *152*
  tables *80*
  walls *21*

L

ladders, as shelves *25*, *26*
Lagerlöf, Selma *134*
lampshades *26*, *36–7*, *82*, *83*
laser cutters 10, *10*
letterpresses 12, *15*, 122,
  124, *125*, 148
Lewandowski, Stef 9
Lewin, Angie 75
lighting

Acknowledgments

A huge thank you to Helen Cathcart for photographing this book so beautifully. Thank you for seeing things the way I did and for being such a brilliant travelling companion. As a fellow photographer, I couldn't have asked for anyone better to work with.

A great big thank you to all the wonderful Makers, who let us into your homes and studios with so much love. It was a complete joy to meet you all and everyone of you inspired me to go home, make things and redecorate my home!

Thank you so much to Nathan Joyce for believing in me and my idea, and to the team at Ryland Peters and Small, particularly to Toni Kay, for all their support and hard work.

I would also like to thank my friends who have been so patient and understanding while I've been working on the book! And my parents, Helen and Philip, for surrounding me with books throughout my childhood and beyond, and for giving me the courage to always follow my dreams.

The most enormous thank you goes to my family; my husband Stef and our four amazing children, Imogen, Oren, Max and Rudi. You are the most creative people in my world, and you all inspire me to make something every day.

And finally, thank you to all of you who follow me, read my blog, come to my workshops and read my book! None of this would be possible without your support and encouragement. You make me smile every day! Now let's all get excited and make stuff!

Love Emily xx